Praise for
Coffee *for* Roses
and C.L. Fornari

"Every gardener needs a mentor. C.L Fornari's *Coffee for Roses* mixes humor and wisdom to dispel many of the most stubborn gardening myths and folklore, while guiding us all to be more successful gardeners."

– Joe Lamp'l, executive producer and host, Growing a Greener World®

"I love garden 'myth busting' – so many old-spouse-tales are in need of debunking. How can you tell what's real and what's not? In her fun and funny new book, expert garden communicator C.L. Fornari helps gardeners tell truth from fiction."

– Ken Druse, award-winning author of over a dozen books on gardening and host of the Ken Druse REAL DIRT radio show

"C.L. Fornari brings a depth of knowledge and passion of expression to all of her many forms of communication and horticultural outreach. Read her and be delighted!"

– Kirk R. Brown, speaker and presenter of "John Bertram Lives!"

"If anyone knows the truth about gardening, it's C.L. Fornari. She has seen and heard it all. What a fun, enlightening read for gardeners of all skill levels and interests."

"There are quite a few Master Gardeners in the U.S. today – there are fewer Garden Masters. C.L. is one of them. It's refreshing to hear her dispel so many of the myths we gardeners have heard for so many years. Brava!"

"In *Coffee for Roses*, C.L. Fornari tells it like it really is. With fact and humor, this well-known garden writer and lecturer has nailed most of the urban garden myths passed along by gardeners. Kudos to her for writing a book that every gardener will value for its wisdom and wit!"

Coffee *for* Roses

...and **70** Other Misleading Myths About Backyard Gardening

Coffee *for* Roses

...and 70 Other Misleading Myths About Backyard Gardening

C.L. Fornari

st. lynn's
press

PITTSBURGH

Coffee for Roses
And 70 Other Misleading Myths About Backyard Gardening

ISBN-13: 978-0-9892688-3-7

Library of Congress Control Number: 2013952969
CIP information available upon request

First Edition, 2014

St. Lynn's Press . POB 18680 . Pittsburgh, PA 15236
412.466.0790 . www.stlynnspress.com

Book design – Holly Rosborough
Editor – Catherine Dees

Photo credits: All photos by the author, with the exception of:
Page 58 – ninjatacoshell (oak leaf), Page 67 – Walter Siegmund (holly leaf), Page 76 – Rosendahl (red slug),
Page 94 – theornamentalist, Page 131 – Linda Tanner (crow); and spot photo art on Pages 2, 6, 20, 32, 38,
56, 78-79, 80-81, 82, 88, 104, 106-107, 108-109, 110, 119, 124-125 and 145.
Page 112 – image courtesy of the Oklahoma Historical Society.

Page 88: The article "An Odd Fertilizer for Plants" is courtesy of
the Virginia Newspaper Project, Library of Virginia, Richmond.

MIX
Paper from
responsible sources
FSC® C016245

Printed in Canada
On certified FSC recycled paper using soy-based inks

This title and all of St. Lynn's Press books may be purchased for educational,
business or sales promotional use. For information please write:
Special Markets Department . St. Lynn's Press . POB 18680 . Pittsburgh, PA 15236

10 9 8 7 6 5 4 3 2 1

FOR MY MOTHER,

JANICE S. ALBERTSON,

WITH THANKS FOR

"THE GREEN THUMBS GENES."

Table of Contents

Introduction

My first experience with a horticultural enterprise was in Muncie, Indiana, when I was nine years old. One humid summer day a friend and I wanted to go into town for ice cream but didn't have any money. We thought about how we might quickly get some cash and decided that we should sell something.

There were several stacks of old clay flowerpots behind our garage, along with a rusty shovel for digging. Perfect! We grabbed several of the pots and filled them with dirt, also from behind the garage, arranging them in my family's Radio Flyer wagon.

Next, we scampered around the adjacent backyards, picking the neighbors' flowers. After stabbing the stems into the pots of dirt, we wheeled our collection door-to-door.

"Would you like to buy a plant? They're only a nickel," we said when someone came to the door. I can only imagine that people thought we were cute because we made several sales – often to the very same neighbors we'd stolen the flowers from in the first place.

Fortunately, over the years I've learned about the importance of root systems and ethics. I've also found that there's always something new to discover. Most subjects are more multifaceted than they initially appear and things are always changing. As we garden we learn to be flexible, and as we work with plants we appreciate how truly complex they are.

I've seen that when it comes to gardening there isn't one right way. Someone can do everything wrong and still be successful, because

The author's entry garden at Poison Ivy Acres on Cape Cod. Among the plants that thrive here are Profusion zinnias, Sedona Coleus, Russian sage and Calamintha.

plants frequently grow against all odds. That said, although the phrase wasn't spoken about gardening specifically, Walt Kelly's Pogo was right. Pogo used to say, "We have met the enemy, and he is us."

We *Homo sapiens* are prone to overreaction, control issues, and downright wackiness. Although most of us aren't depending on the garden for our winter food, if a plant isn't doing well we're likely to panic, leaping into action with no plan or information that allows us to respond appropriately.

We're also stubborn, disposed to thinking that we know best even when our opinions fly in the face of how Mother Nature has grown plants since the first cell photosynthesized. This was, of course, well before our ancestors were walking upright, yet we humans frequently choose to ignore basic ecological principles. Why do we do that?

It appears that we're hardwired to be attracted to the novel: if it's different, we pay more attention. We remember what's unusual, unique. This is probably a good survival strategy; if *Homo sapiens* only noticed the same old same old, the species would have died out the first time a food source disappeared. Perhaps this hardwiring explains why we're more likely to remember odd tips, even if they sound silly, such as using chewing gum for groundhogs or hanging geraniums upside down.

Although one definition of myth is "false belief," another is "an ancient story." The gardening life is full of myths and hand-me-down tips. Some years ago, I started speaking about garden myths, having long been interested in tracking these intriguing bits of lore back to their origins. I began by reading gardening books from the late nineteenth and early twentieth centuries. For the most part, these older books contained commonsense information that bears remembering today. Surprisingly, the most questionable garden advice I was finding actually originated in the mid-twentieth century.

It became clear to me that gardeners over 100 years ago were in many ways much more in touch with natural processes and at peace with the necessity of hands-on effort. Reading the advice in these books and old newspapers was thoroughly enjoyable, especially when the author's personality shone through in the wording, prejudices and the recounting of personal garden experiences.

You'll find some of my own biases and garden encounters in this book. Be forewarned that I have a tendency to make links between the plant world and the rest of modern life. It isn't just in nature that everything is connected to everything else.

I am now many years beyond that nine-year-old who was peddling stolen stems in a wagon, yet I'm still trying to market plants. If you say

that garden writers and speakers are plant pushers, then I'm guilty as charged. I believe that gardening is one of the most life-affirming things we can do.

In addition to beautiful flowers and delicious food, insight, relaxation, inspiration, solace, a good workout, and plenty of laughs can be grown in your backyard, or on the windowsill and terrace. Let's keep our eyes and minds open and keep on planting.

C.L. Fornari

* * *

"If you're taking care of everything perfectly you're not growing enough plants."
– David Burdick

Annuals
&
Perennials

—‿‿‿—

*"Remember that children, marriages,
and flower gardens reflect
the kind of care they get."*

– H. Jackson Browne

Or, in the words of Milton Berle,
"A thing of beauty is a job forever."

1. A perennial garden is less work than an annual planting because the plants come up every year.

"I want a low-maintenance garden," my consultation customer said, "so we should fill my yard with perennials." This client wasn't unique in thinking that a perennial garden is less work. As a novice gardener I too thought that if a flowering plant came up every year it wouldn't require as much effort and attention. Many seasons and gardens later, I now know that a perennial garden is the most high-maintenance flowerbed you can plant.

Not that this stops me from growing and recommending perennials, mind you. I designed a garden for that customer that included shrubs, bulbs and some perennials that are less work. The plants we call herbaceous perennials are desirable not just because they die to the ground and come back from their roots; gardeners love these plants for the kaleidoscope of color they bring to the landscape. A perennial bed is constantly changing through the seasons as the flowers and foliage come and go. Still, this continual show needs frequent and ongoing attention.

> I now know that a perennial garden is the most high-maintenance flowerbed you can plant.

Every plant has a personality, just as people do. Although many plants are called perennials this doesn't mean that they all behave similarly. In fact, I often say that tending perennial gardens is a great deal like being a teacher in a third-grade classroom.

A good elementary school instructor figures out how each of the students will learn best. He or she watches to see the strengths and weaknesses of the pupils, learns about their home lives, and considers how to best train, support and guide them. A teacher might need to work with twenty or thirty different personalities and learning styles while still maintaining order in the classroom.

So it is with perennial gardening. Gardeners learn which plants can be left alone from year to year and which varieties need an annual editing because they spread so quickly. We see that some perennials return reliably and others have a shorter life span. Certain plants are floppy while others remain upright. A few are obnoxious thugs and some are as frail as the petals on their flowers.

To keep a perennial bed looking its best, the gardener must contain the overly vigorous, prop up the floppy, deadhead or cut down the tired, pull or transplant self-sown seedlings, and replace plants that don't thrive. This work continues through the growing season as perennials come into and out of their peak flowering periods.

It isn't just the differences between plant varieties that demand attention from perennial gardeners, however. The task that requires the most ongoing awareness is weed control. Annual gardens are easy because the area is totally cleared in the spring and everything – plants, weeds and annuals – is removed in the fall. In a perennial garden, weeds are constantly looking for an opportunity, and they are sneaky.

Weeds will grow in between peony stems, inside clumps of iris and throughout the Shasta daisies. They'll sprout in the fall and grow all winter. (The #$%@&* chickweed!) Weeds view any little bit of open soil as available real estate, requiring the wise perennial gardener to notice and pull these unwanted invaders several times a year. Yes, mulch will help, but the best weed control is still the gardener's shadow.

In a perennial garden, being there frequently matters. Tending a perennial garden is enjoyable, satisfying work, but it is not low-maintenance.

This beautiful perennial garden looks like it takes care of itself, but in truth the gardener, Joyce Maxner, spends a fair amount of time weeding and editing. Since some plants are fairly restrained but others want to grab as much land as possible, keeping things in balance is a perennial gardener's mission.

The following are some of the perennials that require less maintenance. Remember that all plants tend to be less work when they're planted in their preferred growing conditions. *Note:* when a particular cultivar's name is shown, it's because this is a more carefree variety...other varieties or species may not be the same.

- Big Bang coreopsis (Coreopsis Big Bang Series) zones 5-9, sun
- Calamint (*Calamintha nepeta* spp. *Nepetoides*) zones 5-10
- Catmint (*Nepeta* x *faassenii* 'Walker's Low') zones 4-9, sun
- Cleveland sage (*Salvia clevelandii*) zones 8-10, sun
- Crinum lily (*Crinum* ssp.) zones 8-11, sun
- Daylily (Hemerocallis hybrids) zones 3-10, sun
- Early flowerer sneeze weed (*Helenium* 'Sahin's Early Flowerer') zones 4-8, sun
- False indigo (*Baptisia australis*) zones 3-10, sun
- Hardy hibiscus (*Hibiscus moscheutos*) zones 4-10, sun
- Hosta (*Hosta* ssp.) zone 3-9, pt. shade/shade
- Lady fern (*Athyrium felix-femina*) zones 4-9
- Lily of the Nile (*Agapanthus* spp.) zones 8-11, sun
- Old fashioned bleeding heart (*Dicentra spectabilis*) zones 3-9, pt. sun/pt. shade
- Orange peel Jessamine (*Cestrum* 'Orange Peel') zones 7-9 sun/pt. sun
- Peony (*Paeonia* hybrids) zones 3-7, sun
- Pineapple Popsicle poker plant (*Kniphofia* 'Pineapple Popsicle' and 'Mango Popsicle') zones 6-9, sun
- Purple-leaf bugbane (*Actaea* 'Brunette' or 'Hillside Black Beauty') zones 4-8, pt. sun/pt. shade
- Russian sage (*Perovskia atriplicifolia*) zones 4-9, sun
- Short balloon flower (*Platycodon grandiflorus* 'Early Sentimental Blue' and similar) zones 3-8, sun
- Stoke's aster (*Stokesia laevis*) zones 5-10, sun
- Texas lantana (*Lantana urticoides*) zones 8a-11, sun
- Wall germander (*Teucrium chamaedrys*) zones 6-9 sun
- Yellow hakon grass (*Hakonechloa macra* 'Auerola') zones 5-9 pt. sun/pt. shade

2. Perennials live from year to year and are winter hardy.

Think of all the friends you've had over the years. If you're lucky there are some who've been with you from childhood. There are also those you only vaguely remember and some you've forgotten completely. There have undoubtedly been a few sad disappointments, while others have surprised you with their generosity and the beauty of their spirits. So it is with perennial plants.

We'd like to think of perennials as reliably returning year after year but they can be as varied in constancy as any of life's companions. Most perennials have a typical life span even when grown in optimum conditions, and this will vary depending on location – where the plants are grown.

> Most perennials have a typical life span even when grown in optimum conditions.

In one part of the country a perennial might return every spring, while in another area that same variety behaves as an annual. Gardeners in the Seattle area can grow delphiniums, for example, but even though they're labeled as hardy in much of the Northeast and Midwest,

if you get them back a second year it's a gift from God.

How can a novice gardener know which plants will be truly hardy and which ones might behave like annuals in their landscape? Ask other gardeners, members of an area garden club, or the volunteer Master Gardeners. Just keep it regional; advice that you receive online might not apply to your location. Local gardeners can tell you which perennials will be fair-weather friends and which ones will be your new BFF.

It's no wonder that gardeners fall for these lovely blue delphiniums. But even though their labels claim them to be perennial, in most parts of North America delphiniums need to be grown as annuals. Never mind...if you love them they're worth planting every year.

3. Passalong plants from neighbors or plant sales are a great way to plant a perennial garden.

At first glance a passalong plant makes sense. If other gardeners in the area are growing it successfully, it's likely that you'll be able to grow it too. A dose of reason and reality comes from my friend Stephanie Foster, who is a gardener, photographer and writer. Stephanie once said that she has the following rule: "Never accept a plant someone else wants to give you... there's a reason they have it to give away."

The longer I tend gardens and see landscapes planted by others, the more convinced I am that Stephanie is onto something. Plants that are commonly given away are varieties that spread quickly, self-seed, or need frequent dividing. It's likely that in three to five years you too will be editing, dividing, or even cursing them.

> Passalong plants often become make-work plants.

"But I enjoy gardening," you say. Admittedly, when looking at the garden one plant at a time, that Siberian iris or gooseneck loosestrife might not seem problematic. Once the perennial bed is filled with such plants, however, it's a high-maintenance landscape and even the most dedicated

People love gooseneck loosestrife (Lysimachia clethroides) because the flowers are really lovely. That's the plant's strategy to get invited into the garden. Consider that those beautiful flowers just might be a disguise. Once planted, this perennial behaves like Romans conquering the ancient world. You've been warned.

gardener can become overwhelmed. Passalong plants are usually make-work plants. If your goal is a low-maintenance landscape, avoid them.

Passalong plants also might arrive with undesirable tagalongs. I learned this many years ago when I accepted daylilies from a friend. Hidden in the soil were tiny ticking time bombs: seeds of bishop's weed, also known as goutweed or *Aegopodium*.

Bishop's weed is one of the most invasive perennials I know. Once it starts growing it's extremely difficult to eradicate. I wouldn't be exaggerating much if I said that you need a combination of Agent Orange and nuclear weapons to kill this plant. I avoided such weaponries by moving and leaving this thug behind.

Changing landscapes isn't a workable response for most gardeners, so shunning passalong pests is advisable. Unfortunately, unsuspecting gardeners often don't recognize that a problem perennial has taken root until it is well established.

Of course, there's no guarantee that the plant you purchase at a garden center won't also contain weeds or problematic tagalongs. But it's *more* likely that plants from a home garden will come with stowaway seeds or plants.

So, when a neighbor says, "I'll give you some…" remember Stephanie's rule. Passalong plants are often passalong problems.

Some plants play well with others but some want to take over the world. I love black-eyed Susan, but this garden shows how much they spread. Though rudbeckia makes a great groundcover in sun, the plant will need constant editing in a mixed perennial garden.

4. Ants help peonies open.

If this book were a street map, ants and peonies would thrive at the intersection of Myth and Metaphor. Those who appreciate allegory love this gardening fable, even as gardeners continue to denounce its accuracy. Ants bring peonies into bloom in numerous sermons, motivational speeches and inspirational messages. But in real life? Not so much.

> The ants are only there for a shot of sugar.

Legend says that the peony bud is covered with a protective covering that the ants must eat away before the flower can break open. The truth is that the bud will open on its own, insects or not. The ants are only there for a shot of sugar.

As peony buds develop, they exude a sap that is sweeter than soda. The concentration of sugar in plant juices is between 20 to 25 percent, as compared to 10 percent in colas. It's no wonder that the ants flock to harvest the peony's nectar; but is the plant benefiting from the insects' presence?

Many plants use nectar to draw in pollinators, but some produce sap that isn't related to fertilization. Botanists have studied such extrafloral nectaries for years to determine how they benefit plants and ants. Studies on some

Whether you have ants on your peonies or not, growing a few clumps of this sturdy perennial will provide you with at least one totally extravagant bouquet every summer.

plants (not peonies) showed that the presence of ants prevents other insects and herbivores from damaging flowers or fruit. For other plants, the presence of ants provided no such protection.

It's clear that ants profit from the peony's nectar, but we don't know if the plant has, at some point in history, benefited from the ants. Many of nature's ways remain a mystery, and there are surely useful metaphors in that.

5. Deadhead perennials so they will bloom again.

"You can either deadhead your coreopsis or you can have a life." That's what a friend told Stephanie Cohen, aka The Perennial Diva, when she confessed to deadheading her 'Moonbeam' *Coreopsis* with cuticle scissors. Fortunately, the process of removing old flowers from perennials doesn't need to so meticulous. There are some plants that don't need deadheading at all and there are many that can be dealt with using a shearing tool or hedge clippers.

When thinking about deadheading, it's helpful to remember a plant's purpose in life. Simply put, every plant's mission is to push its genetics into the future. In order to fulfill this purpose, plants that have one short season to live (annuals) need to create as many seeds as possible. The flowers attract pollinators that fertilize the blooms so they create seeds. In an effort to make as many seeds as possible, annuals continue to bloom when old blossoms are removed.

But perennials can slack off a bit on seed making, since they usually come back from their roots the following season. Most perennials have two ways of pushing their genetics forward.

> Snipping off perennial flowers doesn't always stimulate bloom.

And since seed production isn't crucial, snipping off spent perennial flowers doesn't always stimulate bloom.

A few plants flower again if the old flowers are removed, but others do not. Often, however, taking off the spent blossoms improves the look of the garden. There are several ways this can be done. Some plants can be sheared in half or even to the ground. Others can be clipped just below

Some of us meticulously deadhead coreopsis flower by flower, some chop the plant in half in mid-summer, and others leave the plant to its own devices until fall. Take whatever approach suits you the best.

the dead flowers, and a few, such as daylilies, look best if the old flower stems are completely removed.

In order to learn how each perennial is best deadheaded, do some research online or ask other gardeners, but the best teacher is experience. Clip, shear, or cut to the ground and see what happens.

On a plant-by-plant basis, do what makes the overall garden look good and don't get too fussy. In or out of flower, a perennial should be an asset in the landscape and you should have a life.

Some plants need something more drastic than deadheading. This blue and gold spiderwort (Tradescantia 'Sweet Kate') is a good example of a perennial that's better cut to the ground after flowering. When treated that way, space is made for late-summer kale or pansies, and the spiderwort puts up new, fresh foliage for fall.

6. Perennials should be divided by using two garden forks, scissoring them back and forth to pry clumps of roots apart.

Think of all the gadgets that end up cluttering kitchen drawers because they just don't work. Meatball makers, onion choppers and potato nails, to name just a few. They seemed like a good idea, but...

The scissoring fork method of perennial dividing is the garden version of a kitchen gadget that doesn't perform. Nevertheless, for several years this technique was promoted in books and articles as an effective way to tease a plant's roots apart. You can still find illustrations of this on the Internet. There's a reason that this approach was usually shown in a drawing, not a photograph: in reality it's difficult to impossible to make it work.

> It's far more efficient to cut perennials into pieces with a shovel.

Gardeners know how to divide perennials. You stick a shovel or spade into the soil around the plant, cutting into the roots and dirt until you're able to lift all or part of the clump from the ground. If the piece is still too large you slice it again with the same tool. No namby-pamby root separation is needed.

It's far more efficient to make meatballs with your hands, chop onions with a knife, bake nailless potatoes, and cut perennials into pieces with a shovel. Fortunately, there are other uses for garden forks.

When printed in gardening books this myth was often illustrated with drawings. It's no wonder; dividing perennials by scissoring garden forks seems like a good idea but in real life it seldom works.

7. Biennials bloom every other year.

"Do you have odd-year foxgloves?" the customer asked me. I was standing in the perennial section of the garden center and must have looked puzzled because she hurried to explain. "I know that biennials bloom every other year," she said, "and mine flowered last year which was an even number. They'll bloom again next year, I guess, but I'd like to have some that flower in odd numbered years so that I always have them."

> A biennial grows one year, blooms the next, and then it dies.

"Who wouldn't want foxglove in their garden every year?" I agreed, but explained that she misunderstood what biennials do. These plants don't flower every other year; they take two years to complete their life cycle. A biennial grows one year, blooms the next, and then it dies.

I assured her that she didn't need special even or odd year plants. If she loves foxgloves she should just start some from seeds every spring. The young plants will grow over the first season and flower the next.

When these plants are happy they often self-seed, so they might return year after year. But by planting a few beloved biennials every spring, gardeners will know that whether the year is even or odd the flowers will grace their gardens.

Three biennials wandered through this garden for several years. Purple foxglove, yellow verbascum, and white feverfew self-sow and flower in early summer. Because these often seed inside clumps of other plants or in other places where they don't belong, they frequently need transplanting when they're small.

A heavy snowfall insulated the dozens of foxglove plants the winter before this photo was taken. The following June there were foxgloves flowering everywhere on this property.

8. Daffodils need to be deadheaded.

When my husband and I moved to New York's mid-Hudson Valley my mother sent us a daffodil collection as a housewarming gift. I planted the 100 bulbs in the sloped perennial garden by the driveway, and they were true to the package that claimed these were *Narcissus* for naturalizing. Within four years this bed was filled with hundreds of daffodil flowers every spring.

Another gardener told me that I needed to snap off the old flowers because developing

> A daffodil stem photosynthesizes, producing energy that is returned to the bulb.

daffodil seeds robbed the bulbs of energy. As I was doing this, a friend stopped by and criticized my method. "If you just snap off the old flowers and leave the stems it looks ugly," she said, explaining that I should be cutting the entire stalks down. My back didn't like that advice, but for the next ten years I dutifully bent over and clipped those stems to the ground.

After moving to Cape Cod I attended a conference for landscape professionals that was sponsored by our local Cooperative Extension.

Yes, the plant puts energy into making seeds; this is how the plants propagate themselves. Daffodils that are hardy, strong varieties don't suffer from producing seeds.

14

One of the speakers that day, David Burdick, is a daffodil grower from the western part of Massachusetts. After speaking about raising *Narcissus*, and showing slides of his beautiful fields, he called for questions. I innocently asked how he got those thousands of daffodils deadheaded. He laughed at me.

I should have realized that if all of the spent flowers were removed, the grower would never be able to recoup the investment in labor when selling the bulbs. Aside from cost effectiveness, however, David was happy to share the *Narcissus* essentials I needed to know.

It seems that many daffodil varieties are actually sterile and don't produce seeds at all. The *Narcissus* that go to seed have evolved that way and, given favorable growing conditions, the plant usually remains perennial. And finally, I learned that when I was diligently cutting those stems to the ground, *that* was actually detrimental.

A daffodil stem photosynthesizes, producing energy that is returned to the bulb. So in my diligence to do it right, I was really doing more harm than good.

Live and learn. Frankly, it was a relief to discover that this was one back-breaking job I could cross off my to-do

list. Several years later, when I visited Martha Schmidt's cheerful fields of poetica daffodils on Martha's Vineyard, I recalled David's words. Her *Narcissus poetica* are descendants of bulbs planted well over 100 years ago. They are numerous, beautiful, and never deadheaded.

These daffodils cover a field on Martha's Vineyard. They are descendants of some that were planted in the late 1800s by Professor Nathaniel Southgate Shaler, a weekend resident from Boston. Needless to say, no one has been deadheading this field of plants.

Plant red flowers to attract hummingbirds.

If you type "hummingbird feeder" into Google Image, dozens of pictures will appear and most of them will be red. If the body of the feeder isn't red, the nectar tube is likely to be scarlet tipped or framed by a crimson plastic flower. The red color isn't there to entice hungry birds, but to attract the people who are buying a hummingbird feeder.

Hummingbirds also love these pink and white Nicotiana mutibilis, *and the lavender* Agastache 'Blue Fortune' *that grows behind it.*

Research shows that hummingbirds constantly search for nectar-rich flowers but the color of the blooms isn't important. In fact, whether the food-source is a feeder or flowers, the *location* is the chief attractant. If a feeder is moved several feet to another location the birds will come to the original site and, finding no nectar, will fly off to other known feeding areas. They don't look to one side or another for that familiar red plastic.

> The color of the blooms isn't important.

Every year I fill the planters on my deck with blue salvia (*Salvia guaranitica* 'Black and Blue') and whatever peach-flowering *Agastache* my garden center happens to have in stock. Knowing that hummingbirds will return annually to the same location, I'm glad that my *Nicotiana mutabilis* (pink and white) reliably self-seeds and the 'Belgica' honeysuckle (peach and yellow) is perennial and long flowering.

So if scarlet and crimson aren't your favorite colors, don't be concerned. There are plenty of flowers that will keep the airspace around your gardens busier than O'Hare; the hummingbirds will be happy and you'll never see red.

I always plant this blue salvia (Salvia guaranitica 'Black and Blue') in the containers on my deck because it is a hummingbird favorite.

10. Give annuals a fertilizer with a really high middle number to encourage more flowers and add super phosphate to the soil when planting perennials.

As a beginning gardener I was told that if I wanted my annuals and perennials to flower well I should use a fertilizer with a high middle number. Books and articles explained that the three numbers on a fertilizer package stand for percentages of nitrogen, phosphorous and potassium. A high amount of nitrogen would promote leaf growth, and more phosphorous, I learned, would produce roots and flowers.

When I told Chuck Otto, in Technical Services at Ball Horticultural, that popular gardening advice has long recommended using a fertilizer with more phosphorous, his response was succinct. "There is no reason for using a fertilizer with a high middle number now, and there wasn't back then."

"Adding more phosphorous to the soil isn't helping anything." Chuck continued. "Phosphorous is, in fact, a pollutant. It's not necessary and in some cases it's detrimental because you can tie up other materials the plant might need."

In fact, many states either ban or discourage phosphorous use unless it's applied to correct a known deficiency. Since we're all more aware of the environmental consequences of our actions, the days of automatically throwing a handful of super phosphate into a planting hole are clearly over.

In addition to better protection of the ecosystem, we know that the performance of flowering annuals isn't improved by high-phosphorous formulas. I've seen that many of the newer annuals are actually nitrogen hogs; so for confirmation, I went to a company that grows huge amounts of these plants, Proven Winners, and talked with their Director of Product Development, John Gaydos.

"At Proven Winners," John explained, "we know that the plants we bring to the market do best with a higher amount of nitrogen. What we're looking for in a fertilizer for our plants is a ratio of 2 parts nitrogen, .5 phosphorous, and 1.5 potassium. This is because our plants produce the most flowers on new growth, and the best way to keep new growth coming through the season is with a fertilizer that has a higher rate of nitrogen."

> Adding more phosphorous to the soil isn't helping anything.

John went on to describe how many of the newer annuals that are brought to market haven't evolved in a phosphorous-rich environment. "A lot of our plants have originated South Africa and Australia," he said, "where there are very low amounts of phosphorous in the soil. The plants that thrive in those parts of the world have developed without much phosphorous, so it isn't necessary to include it in their fertilizers."

When in doubt, have a complete soil test done so you know what's available naturally. And when growing annuals, provide a complete fertilizer over the summer that encourages new growth with a higher percentage of nitrogen.

This beautiful Proven Winners display garden at Nordic Nurseries in Abbortsford, British Columbia, is planted primarily with annuals. It makes good environmental and practical sense to fertilize such plants with slightly higher levels of nitrogen and lower amounts of phosphorous.

11. Lemongrass repels mosquitos.

When mosquitos are out for blood, humans are not their first choice. It's small comfort, but most mosquito species prefer horses and cattle, while others seek out reptiles or birds. There's also little consolation in knowing that mosquitoes are a food source for the frogs and dragonflies we gardeners love so well. Mosquitoes are a serious annoyance and the diseases they

Get some citronella candles and spray repellants to keep mosquitoes away.

spread are occasionally fatal. It's no wonder that we look for anything that repels this bothersome pest.

Knowing that the scent of citronella wards off mosquitoes, many gardeners plant pots of lemongrass in hopes that this will help. Unfortunately, the species of *Cymbopogon* that produce citronella (*C. winterianus* and *C. nardus*) are not the same plant as the culinary variety (*C. citratus*) that is commonly sold in garden centers.

Ann McCormick, The Herbin' Cowgirl, says that even if gardeners could get their hands on the correct variety (which, by the way, grows up to 6' tall) merely placing one in the garden wouldn't help. Citronella is the oil distilled from the leaves, Ann says, "So it's the juice or sap of the herb that repels insects. Unless you plan on crushing the leaves and

Lovers of Thai food or cross-cultural cooking will insist on planting a lemongrass in their herb garden every summer. The plants get larger when planted in the ground, but if grown in a pot they are fairly easy to bring inside for the winter. This is a must-have herb for cooking or tea, but not for insect control.

smearing them on your body, having the grass on the patio does little to get rid of mosquitoes."

This Texas herb expert goes on to say that there are two other plants that can discourage mosquitoes: tansy and basil. "The down side is that it's also the juice of these herbs that deters insects, so just having them planted nearby has little effect."

Another mosquito myth that Ann would like to slap down is that a citronella-scented geranium (*Pelargonium* x *citronellum*) keeps irritating insects away. Sometimes the plants are even sold with a mosquito prominently pictured on the labels. "This is nothing but a marketing ploy to sell these scented geraniums," Ann fumes.

Here's the real buzz: grow the scented geraniums for potpourri and the lemongrass for Thai cooking, but get some citronella candles and spray repellants to keep mosquitoes away.

Old Mosquito Recommendations Better Left in the Past

Mosquito control at the beginning of the 20th century makes our current interest in insect-repelling plants look environmentally benign.

The section on mosquitoes in *Farm and Garden Rule-Book*, written by L. H. Bailey While and published in 1911, starts off well by acknowledging that, "The chief mode of attack is to *destroy their breeding-places* [italics his]. They breed only in standing water. Draining the breeding-places, or filling them up and emptying all receptacles in which water stands, is the first thing to be considered."

Mr. White adds that any body of water that can't be emptied should be covered with a layer of kerosene oil "so that mosquito larvae may be deprived of air." The author recommends that where aquatic plants are growing, spraying with kerosene will kill the plants. "It should be poured on surface of water in cultivated ponds and spread with a broom or mop."

This and other writings of the period also quote Dr. L.O. Howard and Dr. John B. Smith's advice to control mosquitoes in houses by fumigating with powdered jimson weed (*Datura stramonium*), a poisonous plant that contains dangerous levels of toxic alkaloids.

Should mosquitoes continue to bite after these management attempts, an article in the June 12th, 1912 issue of the *New York Times* offers the following suggestion for mosquito bite relief. "The Rev. R. W. Anderson of Wando, S.C. says that he has found by holding his hand to a hot lamp chimney the irritation of mosquito punctures is instantly relieved."

Save geraniums by hanging them upside down in the basement.

Is there something about a geranium that reminds us of workshop tools that can be hung neatly up on pegboard? Or, being seasonal flowers, perhaps they're reminiscent of Christmas decorations that get packed and stored until next year. "OK, we're done with this for now, let's put it down

> Keep the potted geranium growing in a sunny window.

in the basement until we need it next year."

Yet as far back as the early 1900s, extension bulletins and garden columns have advised treating the *Pelargonium* like laundry on the line. "Shake soil from the roots in the fall and hang the plants upside down in a cool, dark, damp basement or cave."

Few of us have caves these days and no one wants a damp basement, but this lore lives on. And truthfully, sometimes the geraniums live on too, but it's despite this treatment, not because of it. Plants that survive a dormant period of neglect in our garages and basements usually have very thick stems, tubers or corms. Think of the dahlias, begonias and other annuals we pack

This charming building at Tuscan Farms in Abbotsford, British Columbia, makes good use of geraniums as a classic cottage garden annual. It's no wonder that many continue to favor this traditional window box annual and want to keep them from year to year.

Geraniums remain a favorite for mixed annual container plantings; they don't mind drying in between watering and their big, bold flowers contrast nicely with other plants that have smaller blooms.

away like summer sports equipment, only to haul them out the following spring.

Those thick parts of the plant have carbohydrates stored in them that keep the plant alive through the winter. No matter if you put the pot of geraniums in the basement as-is, or pack the stems in newspaper in a paper bag and store them in a cool location, they are likely to make it…although I can't imagine they'll be particularly thrilled with the experience.

I'm guessing that someone was short of space in the root cellar and said, "Oh, just hang them from that nail on the wall and see what happens." Lo and behold, those geraniums lived,

that gardener mentioned it to the neighbors, and these poor plants have been sent down in the dark ever since.

If you're out of room yourself and want to give it a try, by all means do so. What's the worst that can happen? A few stems might die. But if you want larger plants, or more *Pelargoniums*, keep the potted geranium growing in a sunny window. In January or February you can take cuttings off that mother plant and by spring you'll have many happy, healthy geranium starts. These cuttings will be starting to bloom when other gardeners are taking their shriveled, half-dead sticks out of the cellar.

Did You Know...

- Our common window box *Pelargonium* is called a zonal geranium because most have rounded foliage that has a different colored area, or zone, in the center of the leaf. Breeders often select for this colored zone, as it makes the plant even more interesting. Leaf coloration in zonal geraniums is most noticeable in the cool weather of spring and fall.

- Scented geraniums grow quickly and can be pruned back through the growing season. Like most *Pelargoniums*, the pieces taken off are easy to root. Scented geranium leaves

  are often used to make tea, and their washed and dried leaves can be placed in a jar of sugar to flavor it for baking. These plants are also a good choice for capturing the interest of children. There are scented *Pelargoniums* that smell like lemon, ginger, chocolate mint, rose and peppermint, to name just a few.

- One thing more: Scented and ivy *Pelargoniums* don't have stems that are as thick as those on zonal geraniums, so these are less likely to live if pulled out of the soil and hung in the basement.

Vegetables

—m—

*"It is not proposed in this plan
to reserve any space for a vegetable
garden, not only for want of room,
but because it is notorious that
vegetables thus grown are
very expensive and troublesome."*

– *Landscape Gardening,*
by Samuel Parsons, Jr., 1895

*"One of the most life-affirming things
we can do is to plant a vegetable garden.
There is nothing so satisfying as being able
to walk into your own yard and ask,
"What's for dinner?"*

– C.L. Fornari, 2014

13. Grow vegetables on raised beds.

Years ago when I was in Tuscany, I noticed that many gardeners had put bottles on the poles that supported tomato plants. Some had used colorful glass wine bottles while others had clear plastic water bottles on their bamboo stakes. I began asking what purpose these bottles served, and no one could tell me.

Each gardener I asked said that they'd seen others do it and so they started doing the same. One man said, "This is a good question. Why are we doing this?" To this day I have no idea if the first person who stuck bottles on their bamboo stakes did so for ornament, as a bird deterrent, so the pole couldn't poke them in the eye, or for some other reason.

> Raised beds, be they contained by boxes or just mounded soil, aren't for everyone.

I'm reminded of this when I think of how vegetable gardens are planted, because often people tend to copy another's approach without understanding why that design has been used. Some construct raised beds, others pile the earth into tall mounds, and some till soil without changing the grade of the land. Raised beds, be they contained by boxes or just mounded soil, aren't for everyone. Are they a good style of vegetable garden for you? Use this checklist to find out.

Raised, Mounded or Flat?

Reasons to Build Raised Beds

- **Accessibility:** Build raised beds that are two feet tall or taller if you have difficulties getting down to ground level or standing up again. A taller raised bed that is only four feet deep can be tended either side standing up or sitting on the framework.

- **Poor Soils:** If the native soil is heavy clay, rock or beach sand you can build a raised bed and fill it with compost-enriched loam. The worse the drainage is, the taller you'd want your bed of improved soil to be. If possible, turn the native soil and improve with organic matter before placing the raised bed on top.

- **Appearance:** Raised beds can be attractive and complement the architecture of buildings and patios.

- **Construction Speed:** For those in a hurry, a raised bed can be built on top of a lawn without turning the soil beneath, especially if the bed is fairly deep.

- **Defining Space:** A raised bed clearly delineates the garden space where the soil isn't walked on.

- **Soil Improvement:** It's easy to maintain the soil structure in a raised bed by adding layers of organic matter (compost, composted manure, chopped leaves, mulch hay, etc.) annually on the soil surface. This holds in moisture and amends soil from the top down.

In some situations it doesn't make sense to actually raise the vegetable beds. When poor drainage isn't an issue, soil can be highly amended and not walked on, yet kept at ground level.

Reasons to Mound up the Soil

- **Drainage & Expense:** Mound soil if you have clay soils or poor drainage and the construction of framed, raised beds isn't possible. Using native soil is less expensive than building beds and importing loam.

- **Local Climates:** Mound soil for faster warming of the land in the spring or to channel water where heavy downpours are likely to occur.

Reasons to Plant on Flat Ground

- **Flexibility:** If you are new to vegetable gardening, avoiding raised beds and mounded soil saves you extra work at the outset. The garden can easily be turned back into lawn or other plantings should you decide that a vegetable garden isn't for you.

- **Freshly Turned Soil:** If you are less than attentive about weed control you might want to hire someone to till your garden every spring and fall. Although this exposes weed seeds that are likely to germinate, it also gives you a "fresh start" every season. Flat gardens are usually easier to turn with a gasoline-powered tiller.

- **Cost Cutting:** Building raised beds can be expensive. You will need to purchase the framing materials and soil and perhaps hire someone for the construction.

- **Raised Beds Don't Have to be Raised:** You can have the advantages of intensive planting and no-turn soil in a flat area. Mark off beds that can be tended from each side and then don't walk in that area. Turn the soil in this area and mix in compost deeply, but from then on amend the soil from the top down without turning. Plant intensively, mulch and hand-pull any weeds that appear.

* * *

From *Cyclopedia of American Horticulture*, 1902, by L.H. Bailey, Professor of Horticulture at Cornell:

"The old-time home vegetable-garden was generally unsuited to the easy handling of the soil and to the efficient growing of the plants. Ordinarily it was a small confined area in which horse tools could not be used. The rows were short and close together, so that finger work was necessary. The custom of growing corps in small raised beds arose, probably because such beds are earlier in the spring than those that are level with the ground.

With the evolution of modern tillage tools, however, it is now advised that even in the home-garden finger-work be dispensed with as much as possible."

This is one of the many gardens we saw in Tuscany where bottles were placed on top of bamboo canes. When glass wine bottles were placed on stronger supports the result was ornamental. These plastic bottles are less attractive, especially in such a pastoral landscape.

14. Squash, cucumbers and pumpkins should be planted on mounds of soil.

We all know the difference between "in" and "on," but when it comes to planting vegetables, gardeners have overlooked the distinction. For years, my husband and I piled up the soil in our veggie garden and planted four or five squash seeds on top of that mound. We were mounding the dirt because the seed packets said to plant squash and cucumbers "in hills."

Using this method of planting wasn't very satisfactory; it was hard to keep the seeds and sprouts moist because the water ran down the incline so quickly. The roots of the young squash plants also dried more rapidly, since this small pile of dirt was more exposed to the air. These difficulties could have been avoided had we been paying attention. The instructions said *in* hills, not *on* them. What a difference one letter makes!

Hills is actually an old agricultural term for a group. After reading that one definition of "hill" is *"several seeds or plants planted in a group rather than a row,"* I had a Homer Simpson moment: "D'oh!" The instructions were telling me to plant the seeds in a cluster, not on a raised mound.

> The instructions were telling me to plant the seeds in a cluster, not on a raised mound.

In many areas it's even advantageous to dig a depression when planting squash. It's easy to keep small seedlings moist by filling that shallow bowl with water. This is especially helpful in regions that have well-drained soil. A depression can also be covered with the floating row cover that's sold at garden centers. This creates a greenhouse-like protection in cool spring weather and shields young plants from insects.

Gardeners who deal with heavy clay and periodic, pouring rains might want to keep planting on mounded soil, but most growers can just group their seeds. And those with sandy soils or cool spring weather will find advantages to planting their *hills* in *valleys*.

This gardener took the "mounds" myth way too seriously!

15. Marigolds keep bugs out of the vegetable garden.

Did you ever play the party game called *Telephone?* The first person whispers a sentence or two into the ear of the next individual, and the message gets murmured around the circle, from one to the next. By the time the original communication has made the rounds of partygoers it bears little resemblance to what the first person said.

When it comes to marigolds in the vegetable patch, gardeners have been playing *Telephone* for years. Noting that for centuries farmers in India have grown marigolds in with vegetables, researchers in the late 1930s began testing whether the genus *Tagetes* controls insect problems.

Those first studies showed a few species of marigolds were effective at controlling *certain* root-knot nematodes, a microscopic worm that attacks plants in warm parts of the country. But by the time this information made the rounds from gardener to gardener it had been transformed into "Marigolds keep bugs away."

Since the original studies were done, many tests of marigolds and nematodes have been conducted with mixed results. In general these

> Tests show no benefit from inter-planting marigolds.

tests show no benefit from simply inter-planting marigolds with other crops. Some experiments showed suppression of particular nematodes when cover crops of specific marigolds were turned into the soil. But no wide scale deterring of general insects has been seen.

Nevertheless, my husband and I start marigold seeds every spring and plant this cheerful flower in our vegetable gardens. After over forty years of gardening, for us the smell of tomato, basil, and marigold foliage is synonymous with summer. As my husband says, "At this point, it's *traditional.*" And so we party on.

For many of us, the scent of marigold foliage is as indicative of summer as the fragrance of tomato and basil foliage. Grow this cheerful annual for ornament or edible flowers, if not for pest control.

16. Companion planting helps plants grow better.

"I've heard that green beans like squash," a friend told me, "but I don't have space to grow both. How do beans feel about tomatoes and basil?" I felt like we were back in high school deciding who would be invited to her party. Do some plants "love" each other? Are there really veggies that have BFFs?

Many scientists say that a better name for grouping plants is intercropping, not companion planting. They believe that the term "companion planting" is too anthropomorphic and leads to false expectations about guaranteed benefits or disadvantages of putting one plant near another.

Tales of companion planting have led people to believe that there might be magic plant combinations that prevent insect or disease damage. While planting a "trap crop" will sometimes draw insects or small animals away from plants they might ordinarily eat, when it comes to hungry critters there are no guarantees.

> It's usually a matter of cultural preferences or resources.

Secondly, gardeners worry about unintentionally combining plants that actually hate each other. But if one plant doesn't do well in the company of another it's usually a matter of cultural preferences or resources.

Do plants have cliques like we did in high school? Not really, although there are combinations that work well because of the size and shape of how plants grow. You could combine lettuce with a tall plant such as Brussels sprouts, so the salad grows underneath. But the lettuce planted along this row of chard is getting covered and overwhelmed by the larger vegetable, so these aren't good companions.

One plant might like damp soil while another prefers it dry, so these probably won't thrive right next to each other. In other cases one plant might use most of the available resources. It's often hard to grow flowers under a maple tree, for instance, because the tree's canopy and roots are so thick. The leaves take all the sunlight and the roots absorb most of the water and nutrients.

There are a few plants that produce substances that seem to inhibit the growth of some other plants. Black walnut trees and the juglone that they produce are often cited as an example of such allelopathy. But studies to measure how black walnuts suppress other plant growth have shown mixed or contradictory results, so even this example isn't certain.

The bottom line is that gardeners should group plants according to the growing conditions they prefer, keeping in mind how these plants mature. Tall, thin eggplants would be fine to place among shorter lettuce, for example, since the lettuce won't mind a bit of shade and they won't crowd each other out. Eggplant and broccoli, however, can't be planted too closely because they grow to a similar size and will compete for space and light.

Part of the fun of gardening is experimenting to see what works in our gardens. Fortunately, we can usually do this without worrying about enigmatic combinations that might cause problems.

Growing a diversity of species is smart because every growing season brings assorted difficulties and blessings, so it's in our best interest to invite many plants to our garden party.

The Three Sisters Garden

The most well known version of intercropping is probably the "three sisters garden." Native American farmers have successfully used this blend of corn, pole beans and squash for ages. The beans are nitrogen fixing, so supply this essential element for the nutrient-hungry corn. The squash vines shade the ground, preserving moisture and preventing weed growth. The corn provides supports for the beans to climb, so these don't get overwhelmed by the squash.

This group planting works well, although Arizona resident Dave Morris remembers learning an alternate version of how corn, beans and squash came to be grown together. One of Dave's aunts used to say that it all came about because Corn didn't know who she should marry, Bean or Squash. So she decided to live with them both to see who would make the best mate. After growing together over many summers, Corn decided to marry Bean. She'd learned that he would cling to her, while Squash was prone to wandering.

17. We must remove the "suckers" on tomato plants.

Searching through farm and garden columns from the late 19th and early 20th centuries tells us two things. First, that pruning shoots from tomato plants has long been a practice to hasten harvest and control the size of plants. Secondly, that home tomato growing has been a competitive sport for years; people love being the first on the block to harvest ripe fruit.

Gardeners are frequently told that the small shoots that grow between the main tomato stem and side branches should be removed. Since these are commonly called "suckers," the implication is that they somehow draw energy away from fruit production. This isn't true.

A 1919 issue of *The New York Sun* records the common thinking that such tomato shoots drain something from the plant. In a column attributed to *F.C.S., Pennsylvania,* the author reports, "When I was young I had to help my father in the garden. He taught me how to take the suckers from tomato plants. Showed me how they grew from the base of the plant – tender

These small shoots are commonly called "suckers," although they do not drain the plant's resources. In fact, on indeterminate types of tomatoes the suckers will grow into branches that flower and bear fruit.

little shoots of or sprouts full of sap – which took strength from the main plant."

Although it's a myth that these stems rob vigor from tomato plants, the practice of pruning off suckers does produce fruit that is slightly earlier and larger. An article in an 1879 issue of the *Shenandoah herald* published in Woodstock, Va., explains that pinching the tops and secondary shoots hastens the maturity of the first fruits. It also mentions that tomatoes were commonly grown sprawled over large areas of ground.

"In small gardens," the paper reports, "where space is limited, a greater quantity of fruit can be obtained by elevating the branches of the plant from the ground with brush or on frames made for the purpose. But for market on a large scale this extra labor is not advised."

In 1904, Guy Elliot Mitchell, a garden writer whose work was published in newspapers across the country, also wrote about the space that tomatoes occupy. He said that "suckers will appear in the axil of each leaf until a vigorous plant will have twenty or more branches, the larger ones having branches of their own, and the whole plant spreading over an area of 10 or 12 square feet." Mitchell was impressed by another space-saving option. He reported that in some parts of the country farmers were beginning to place their tomato plants more closely together, clip off the suckers, and tie the growing plants to stakes "with ordinary white strings."

These days, most home gardeners grow tomatoes vertically, although not everyone pinches the suckers off. Tomatoes labeled as "indeterminate" continue to grow and produce new flowers and fruit though the summer while "determinate" types make one concentrated flower and fruit production. On indeterminate varieties, those suckers will eventually flower and bear fruit. So, if you don't need an earlier harvest, leaving the suckers alone will produce more tomatoes.

Those who want to one-up the neighbors, however, might want to get out the snips. In 1919, *F.C.S. Pennsylvania* went on to say that after removing these small shoots, "My first ripe tomatoes were picked fully ten days before my neighbors." Then this author admitted to taking great pleasure in sending a few of the biggest fruits next door. "They could not understand how it happened, for all the conditions apparently seemed alike. I explained, but it was not appreciated."

> The practice of pruning off suckers does produce fruit that is slightly earlier and larger.

18. The soil in vegetable gardens needs to be turned every year.

In the 1960s, my mother stopped turning the soil in her vegetable garden. The neighbors continued to till the gardens next to hers with plow and Rototiller, but Mom's was no longer touched. She'd begun to use a mulching method laid out in Ruth Stout's book *How To Have A Green Thumb Without An Aching Back*. Using this no-till method the garden's dirt is never turned but is covered with permanent layers of organic mulch, such as hay or leaves.

> Turning soil always exposes weed seeds to light, triggering their germination.

Freshly tilled soil has signaled new beginnings for centuries. Using shovels, plows or home tillers, vegetable gardeners have worked in soil amendments and turned under weeds for so long that people have come to believe that this is a necessity. But since the publication of Stout's book in 1955, many people have decided to alter their thinking instead of the soil.

There are several advantages to no-till gardening. Ruth Stout's focus was less work. Turning soil takes muscle power. In his book *Weedless Gardening*, Lee Reich lists avoiding weeds as another reason not to till. Turning soil always exposes weed seeds to the light, triggering their germination. Less disruption means fewer pesky weeds to deal with.

Other reasons to leave the ground intact include less alteration of natural microorganisms and soil structure, which better imitates nature's processes; no one is plowing in the woods and meadows where organic matter rots

At the Rodale Institute in Kutztown, Pennsylvania, they experiment with no-till methods for home gardeners and farmers. In addition to self-guided tours of their demonstration gardens this non-profit group has a variety of educational materials available on their website.

from the top down. Finally, avoiding soil compaction is another compelling argument not to till. If selected areas aren't walked upon, the soil isn't compressed and this allows roots to grow more quickly.

I'm not arguing that everyone should be planting no-till gardens. We own a tiller and my husband turns our vegetable garden every spring. Turned soil warms faster where spring weather is cool, and organic amendments break down more quickly.

But, from Ruth Stout's heavily mulched vegetable beds to Pat Lanza's *Lasagna Gardening*, there are several other ways to approach growing good food. When it comes to turning or not turning soil, gardeners have options and can decide which method works best for them.

How much work it takes to turn soil is a matter of perspective, as this article from the March 20, 1917 edition of *The Washington Times* shows. The title makes reference to a poem by John Greenleaf Whittier, wherein Maud Muller, a country girl, falls for a local judge but ends up marrying a farmer and working the land.

✤ Suffrage Maud Mullers ✤
Woman's Party Hopes to Pay Rent With Vegetable Garden

By converting the front of the quaint old headquarters on Lafayette Square into a garden of purple, white and gold flowers, the National Woman's Party will keep its colors before the public all summer long. But in a side garden, screened from the public by a brick wall with iron spikes on the top of it, the soil has been turned into a vegetable garden for the raising of onions, potatoes and other products. By the sale of these the Woman's Party hopes not only to pay its rent but to make some money for campaign purposes as well.

The secret leaked out today, when Mrs. S.P. Martin, the only woman florist in Washington, began poking holes in the yard of the Lafayette Square headquarters.

Expect Crop To Pay Rent

A passing reporter was attracted by so much feminine energy, and inquired why all the excavating. Then was unfolded the plan of floriculture for the front portion of the property.

"Fine," said the newspaper man, "but how about a vegetable garden? Are you going to have one?"

Mrs. Martin looked at him pityingly.

"Do you think we'd overlook that with potatoes worth more per pound than violets? I should say not. We expect our potato and onion crop to pay the rent, and they're going to do it, too, because we women are going to dig this garden and look out for it all by ourselves. No mere man shall enter the sacred precincts, not even with a spade."

Suffrage Maud Mullers

The reporter saw a vision of a corps of suffrage Maud Mullers, and glanced at the brick wall with its iron spikes that hides the site of the proposed vegetable garden from prying eyes.

"Digging's pretty hard work for a woman," he ventured.

Mrs. Martin gazed at him sympathetically. Then:

"My dear young man, if you had ever worked for suffrage you would consider digging a garden pure recreation."

19. For sweeter tomatoes, add sugar to the soil or water with sugar water.

I was working in the garden center one spring when one of the cashiers radioed out to the nursery. "There's someone on the phone who wants to know if we sell mara- schino cherry trees," she called. I explained that these were a preserved, sweetened fruit made from a few types of cherries. But a joking co-worker said, "Tell her you can use any cherry tree…you just have to add sugar and coloring to the drip irrigation."

What if we could flavor the water to sweeten vegetables or fruit? We could develop all sorts of complex flavor combinations. Think of irri- gating the tomato plants with bacon water in order to make a pork-free BLT! There could be bubblegum-flavored spinach to tempt children who hate vegetables. I guess we're fortunate that it's not that simple.

The flavor of a tomato is determined by its chemical composition and this is largely estab- lished by the plant's genetics. Recent studies have shown that it's the complex blend of sugars, acids, and several volatile molecules that char- acterize a good-tasting tomato. In other words,

> The flavor of a tomato is determined by its chemical composition.

the combination of taste *and* smell creates the perception of sweetness in our brains.

Vegetable gardeners have long noted that certain varieties of tomatoes are sweeter. Interest- ingly, the taste of the same type of tomato varies from region to region. Even the way the fruit is raised will affect the flavor. Some have noticed that tomatoes picked after a heavy rain aren't as sweet. Finally, even though it sounds counter-

The sweetness of tomatoes is largely determined by genetics but the taste of any type can also vary according to where and how it was grown. These heirloom Virginia Sweets and hybrid Sungold varieties are consistently the sweetest tomatoes grown in the Fornari garden.

intuitive, a slight amount of salt might actually make this fruit sweeter; in many parts of the world tomatoes are irrigated with seawater, which seems to increase fruit sugars.

Sugar not only doesn't get absorbed into fruits, it can slow the growth of plants. Research on applying sucrose to crops has shown that this can result in a kind of reverse fertilization.

Sugar water increases the amount of carbon in the soil, tying up soil nitrogen and resulting in smaller plants.

Those searching for the sweetest tomato should start by asking local vegetable gardeners which varieties they prefer. Experimentation is part of the fun: plant several types and start tasting.

Did You Know...

- Tomatoes have much more flavor if they are kept out of the refrigerator. For this reason ripen tomatoes on the kitchen counter and eat the entire fruit after cutting.

- Mulch around your tomato plants can increase fruit production. Gardeners have traditionally used mulch for moisture retention and weed control, but an added benefit is the increase in numbers of tomatoes grown. Studies show that mulching around tomato plants with either organic mulches or plastic results in higher yields. In general, organic mulches result in greater fruit production. Those using no-till garden methods may find their crops delayed since organic mulches keep soil cooler in the spring.

- Studies in the 1980s and 1990s demonstrated that tomato plants mulched with red plastic sheeting produced more fruit than those grown over black plastic mulch. Later research shows that red plastic influences the taste and size of other crops as well. Basil plants grown with red mulching produced larger leaves. Strawberry fruit size and flavor were improved by red plastic mulching as well: berries grown over a red plastic were 20% larger and had higher sugars and improved flavor and aroma.

- Whenever possible, harvest garden-grown vegetables and fruit shortly before they are to be consumed. A freshly picked vegetable has so much more flavor than one that has been stored for days before cooking.

20. Bend the tops of onion plants to make larger onions.

Sometimes we humans can't leave well enough alone… we just *have* to help even when assistance isn't necessary. This is one explanation for the belief that onion leaves and stems should be pushed over before harvest.

> Most onion tops bend naturally when they're mature.

Most onion tops bend naturally when they're mature, but this hasn't been enough for gardeners through the years. People have been advised to roll barrels over their onion crops, push them with the topside of a garden rake, or bend them down with their hands.

I found mention of all of these techniques in gardening books from the 1890s on. Some claimed that as a result the bulbs would be larger; other sources offered no particular reason for the practice.

In fact, it's day length and temperatures that influence an onion bulb's formation. Early in the season, the onion is in its juvenile stage and just grows leaves. Once the days become long and warm enough, they'll start to form bulbs. The exact hours of daylight needed vary from variety to variety.

After the bulb is formed, the necks naturally get weak and the tops fall over. This is the gardener's cue that the onions should be harvested.

If dug before any of the onion tops have bent, the bulbs are likely to be smaller and not as long lasting when stored. If left in the garden too long, however, onions become mushy and prone to rot.

Most onion plants will bend around the same time, but the gardener doesn't have to wait for all the plants to fall over. If over a quarter of the onion crop has turned down, all of the onions can be considered mature. They can then be harvested and either left on the surface of the soil for a few days or placed somewhere dry to cure before storage.

No one has bent these onion tops over, but most are naturally falling down as the plant matures.

21. You can't plant pumpkins in the garden with squash because they'll cross-pollinate and you'll get "squmpkins."

"I didn't get any zucchini squash this year because of my @#$$%! neighbor," John said. When I asked what the problem was, John shook his head and said something about squmpkins.

"Squmpkins?" I asked.

"Yes," came the grumbled reply. "My neighbor planted pumpkins in his garden, which is just on the other side of the fence. They must have crossed with my summer squash because I have something that's round, yellow-orange, and nothing like a zucchini."

> Most plants only cross with other plants in the same species.

This disgruntled gardener might have had a mystery squash, but it wasn't his neighbor's fault. It's true that a pumpkin flower might pollinate a zucchini blossom. That's because pumpkins and zucchinis, along with acorn squash, gourds, among others, are all varieties of *Cucurbita pepo*. They are in the same genus and species, so they can cross-pollinate.

The results of that pollination are only seen in the children of that cross, however. The seeds inside the fruit might produce John's squmpkins, but the crop itself would be true pumpkins or zucchini.

Most plants only cross with other plants in the same species, although some cross-pollination does occur between plants in the same genus. Rarely a plant will cross with another in a different but related genus. The bottom line for vegetable growers is that they don't have to worry that their tomatoes will cross with the sweet corn, but those who save seed from year to year will need to be aware of which plants are prone to crossing.

When we plant Zephyr hybrid seeds in our vegetable garden we're assured of getting this distinctive yellow and green summer squash.

So how did John get squmpkins? Several things might have happened. If John purchased seed, there might have been the wrong seed in the packet. This is rare but it's been known to occur. If John saved his own seed from squash grown in previous seasons, there might have been other *Cucurbita pepo* in the neighborhood that crossed with his zucchini. Then when he planted that seed he grew the children from two different parents.

Secondly, if John plants summer squash in the same location every year, or puts his vegetable refuse in compost that gets spread on the garden, it's possible that a cross was made in past years and self-seeded. Seeds can survive in the garden or compost and go on to sprout in coming seasons. Many gardeners have noticed random vegetable plants growing from a compost pile or the areas where compost was spread.

No matter how these plants arrived, I advised him to let the mystery squash grow large and carve them as people do pumpkins. Giving them faces that grin or glower could be horticultural therapy for a frustrated gardener.

When Squash Don't Produce

Most summer squash are known for generating more zucchini than one family can use. But occasionally there are plants that don't produce much fruit and gardeners wonder why. Here is some information for those who find themselves with too few zucchini.

- Squash produce male and female flowers on the same plant, but they often make more male flowers than female. Since the plant may produce three or more male flowers before any female flowers are formed, gardeners might assume that their plants only produce males.

- Learn to tell the difference between male and female flowers. The males tend to have thinner, straighter stems while the females are slightly swollen just beneath the petals. Once you know you have both, you can decide if the lack of pollination is the problem.

- Summer squash plants are insect pollinated. So, near your vegetables plant annuals or perennials that attract pollinators. *Rosa*, *Nepeta*, *Calamintha*, *Zinnias* and most herbs are just a few of the plants that attract bees to the garden.

- Planting several squash plants increases the odds that you'll have male and female flowers in bloom at the same time, and therefore better pollination.

- Should you decide to hand pollinate your squash flowers, do so in the morning. Use a finger or small paintbrush to move pollen from the male flowers to the stigma of the female.

22. Vegetable gardens have to be in the backyard.

I am not a garden historian, but my guess is that the convention of putting vegetable gardens in the backyard was a statement about wealth and class. Having a front yard where no crops or livestock are kept says to the world, "I am so well off that I can devote this huge space to something impractical."

In *Horticulture in the North* by D. W. Buchanan, published in 1907, the author says something similar: *"About many farms and rural homes little patchy gardens are seen, worked up by hand. Vegetables planted in raised*

> On many properties the sunniest place is the front yard.

beds, often in front of the house. The approach to the front of the house is sometimes between rows of currant bushes. This plan entails unnecessary labor and is an eye-sore to a person of refined tastes. The fruit and vegetable garden should not be in front of the house."

I have to admit that reading this brought Steve Martin's voice into my head: "Well *excuse* me!"

Fast-forward over 100 years to a time when the trends have changed and even those of refined tastes are growing their own. People

of all incomes are interested in fresh, safe food and edible landscaping is coveted. Terms such as "urban farming" and "foodie" are everywhere

The residents of this summer cottage have decided that a front yard filled with herbs and veggies is preferable to a lawn. Although the beds aren't raised, they are edged with timbers to keep the soil and the clamshell mulching separated.

and the interest in growing vegetables is as popular as it was in the time of the Victory Gardens of World Wars I and II.

Although some still prefer to locate their vegetable gardens in back of the house, practicality currently rules. On many properties the sunniest place is the front yard, so this is where vegetables should be cultivated. Sunny side yards, rooftops, balconies, and community gardens/allotments are also perfect. Look for places that receive at least six hours of dead-on sun, including the noon hour, and start planting.

Vegetables need to grow where the sun is.

Did You Know...

The non-profit organization Kitchen Garden International offers an on-line garden planner that is fun and easy to use. Lay out your garden space and see how many plants you can grow. This is particularly useful for those who have never grown veggies before, and don't know how much space the mature plants will fill.

This planner automatically draws in each variety in appropriate sizes and tells you how many plants will fit in that location. http://gardenplanner.kgi.org/

Some localities still have zoning regulations forbidding front-yard vegetable gardens. Check on local laws before investing a great deal of time and effort constructing your beds, and perhaps organize to get these rules changed.

Enduring Wisdom

An article titled *Vegetables In Home Garden*, published in 1921 in *The Breckenridge News* from Cloverport, Kentucky, is timely today. It was subtitled, All Kinds Should Be Planted; Food Value of Vegetables is Necessary to One's Diet, and the article points out that the better vegetables taste the more likely we are to eat them:

"One of the reasons that many people have to a great extent cut vegetables from their diet is that they have been unable to get fresh vegetables and did not relish stale ones. The individual home vegetable garden planted either in the backyard, or a convenient piece of land, not only solves the problem of supplying the family with vegetables at low cost and in abundance, but guarantees their freshness."

23. Planting tomatoes with eggshells in the hole will prevent black scabs on the bottom of the fruit.

Guy Clark nailed it when he wrote the song *Homegrown Tomatoes*. "There's just two things that money can't buy: true love and homegrown tomatoes."

It's no wonder then that gardeners get discouraged if they find ugly black scabs on the bottom of their fruit. This is blossom end rot and it happens to most tomato growers eventually. The scab may be unsightly, but once it's removed the rest of the tomato is usually still edible.

> The latest research indicates that blossom end rot isn't related to a lack of calcium in the soil.

For years, it's been thought that there is a connection between this condition and calcium, so it's understandable that people made the leap from blossom end rot to eggshells. In fact, in the rush to prevent growing scabby tomatoes, gardeners have advised putting eggshells, Epsom salt, calcitic lime, and even Tums in the tomato patch. However, all of these, as well as calcium sprays, are a waste of time.

The latest research indicates that blossom end rot isn't related to a lack of calcium in the soil. Researchers are now saying that calcium isn't the primary or single factor that leads to this problem. Stress, from a variety of situations, seems to be at the heart of this difficulty.

The most common cause of stress for tomato plants is uneven watering. Allowing the plants to dry in between soakings is frequently the culprit, especially for tomatoes grown in pots or raised beds.

Other stresses include excess water, heat or cold, dry soil, or too much fertilizer. When plants are young they are less able to handle such extremes, so a few tomatoes might be scabby at first while the fruit produced later is unblemished.

Although eggshells won't hurt your plants they, and other sources of calcium, won't prevent blossom end rot. If a homegrown tomato is your definition of true love, keep your plants as disturbance-free as possible and don't stress about calcium.

Tips for Stress-free Tomatoes

- Mulching around tomato plants will help preserve an even level of moisture. Soaker hoses can be laid down first, underneath the mulch, to provide a good soaking irrigation directly into the soil.

- Water tomatoes thoroughly but less often, to encourage deep root systems. In most climates it's not necessary to water every day. Because soil quality and temperatures vary it's impossible to provide one standard guideline for the ideal length and frequency of irrigation. Gardeners should feel the soil or dig down a several inches to determine if the ground is moist or dry.

- Container grown tomatoes might need watering in the morning and late afternoon, especially in hot weather. Check pots and boxes frequently for signs of drying. Drench containers well, let a few minutes go by and then drench them again. Once the soil is well hydrated, don't let your pots or boxes sit in saucers of water, as this will keep the roots too wet.

- Fertilizing should be done regularly in less concentrated applications. Do not exceed recommended dosage, especially for container grown plants. Too much fertilizer of any sort can be stressful.

This myth is a good example of how we can always learn something new about plants and gardening. Even though I knew that eggshells wouldn't decompose quickly into the right form of calcium to help tomatoes, for years I believed that a lack of calcium was the cause of blossom end rot on this fruit. But research has recently shown that a lack of calcium isn't to blame for black-scabbed fruit at all.

Plant peppers with a few matchsticks under each plant.

*W*hat does it take to ignite a myth? In the late 1980s someone decided to give pepper plants a "hot foot," because that's when this invention first appeared in print. Repeated in gardening books in the early 1990s, this advice continues to flare up online today.

The rationale given ranges from the sulfur making soil acidic to the plants responding to phosphorous in the matchsticks. Modern matches do contain phosphorous but little to no sulfur. No matter what they're made from, however, it's hard to imagine how the small amount of combustible material at the end of a tiny strip of wood or paper could alter growing conditions significantly. Moreover, if a few are put in the bottom of a planting hole, a pepper plant's roots will rapidly grow well beyond that small area.

> Certain myths seem to live on despite all common sense.

Certain myths seem to live on despite all common sense. Maybe they spark our sense of whimsy. Possibly they strike a desire to find small flickers of truth or embers of wisdom in odd suggestions. Or perhaps we are just burning to believe that inexpensive objects can kindle greater growth.

Hot foot! Where there's smoke there may be fire, but where peppers are grown you don't need matches.

Peppers love full sun, warm soil, and a fairly long growing season. If you live in the north country, be sure to start your pepper plants early.

Growing Great Peppers

If you're starting your own pepper plants from seed, begin early. Sow peppers indoors in a warm place 10 to 12 weeks before you plan to put them outdoors.

Grow peppers where the plants will get 6 hours or more of sun. Plant in well-drained soil that is slightly acidic, measuring between 6.0 and 6.8. Since this is an ideal pH level for most vegetables, you can plant peppers next to tomatoes and other common home crops successfully.

In northern areas, covering the soil with dark plastic or compost can help bring the soil temperatures up in the spring. Peppers are sensitive to cold; don't plant them in the garden too early. Wait until the nighttime temperatures are reliably above 60°F before planting peppers in the garden.

If space allows, grow several plants in order to have an abundant harvest. Let some fruit ripen on the plants but harvest others a bit early and let them ripen on the kitchen counter. If all the fruit is left on the plants to ripen, the flowering and pepper production may slow.

As with most vegetables, keeping an even level of moisture in the soil around peppers will produce continuing growth. A good strategy for peppers and other veggies is working compost into the soil before planting and mulching – and doing deep soakings less often (instead of daily sprinkling or hand watering).

Pepper plants can be a bit brittle. Support the plants with stakes as needed and harvest peppers with a sharp knife to prevent damage to the stems.

These Sweet Heat peppers from Burpee are a great blend of spicy and sweet. They were incredibly productive when I grew them in a pot on my sunny deck, even though there were no matches mixed in the potting soil.

Shrubs, Trees
&
Vines

---᠁---

"The true meaning of life is to plant trees,
under whose shade you do not expect to sit."

– Nelson Henderson

25. Plant roses with coffee grounds/ banana peels/eggshells.

Did your mother tell you to put coffee grounds, banana peels or eggshells around your roses? She's not alone…people have been placing their breakfast remains around roses for decades.

I found mention of putting eggshells around roses in a Perrysburg, Ohio, newspaper from 1856. *The Philadelphia Public Ledger* from March 7, 1916 advises readers to "Save your coffee grounds, dry them and put around your roses with equal parts of soot."

Mom and these columnists weren't giving *bad* advice, but it's just not all-important or complete. Coffee grounds are fairly rich in nitrogen. Banana skins are high in potassium, and eggshells are predominantly made of calcium carbonate. All of these elements can be found elsewhere, however, and may even be naturally present in your soil.

Roses *are* heavy feeders and they appreciate a higher rate of fertilizer and organic matter. But a balanced, organic fertilizer feeds plants more quickly and is less hit-or-miss when it comes to nutrients. And for organic matter, those who don't drink coffee or eat bananas and eggs can amend soil with other materials such as composted manure.

Sure, you can toss coffee grounds and the like around your rose bushes. But if you don't like the garden to look like a garbage dump, or if you're tired of hearing the crows scream "Eggshells! Eggshells! Eggshells!" as they swoop toward your roses at five a.m., place your kitchen scraps (but not meat or cheese) into a compost bin. Once this has broken down, use it to top-dress the soil around your plants.

> A balanced, organic fertilizer feeds plants more quickly.

Although there's no magic here, if you choose to listen to your mother, place those coffee grounds, eggshells and banana peels around roses under a thin layer of mulch. This will keep the garden looking neat as these organics break down. As your mom might have said, "It couldn't hurt."

Did You Know…

- Coffee grounds do not acidify soils. Since the acid in coffee beans is water-soluble, most of it seeps into our cups and pots.

Brewed coffee grounds are already close to pH *neutral*, as is finished compost.

- Coffee grounds that haven't been composted are considered high in nitrogen but they are not a good fertilizer. When placed directly into the soil, this nitrogen isn't absorbed by plants but is used by the bacteria that assist in decomposition.

- Although eggshells are rich in calcium (an average of 2.2 grams per shell) it would take many shells and several years to begin to influence a soil deficient in this mineral. Calcium carbonate also has poor solubility and this makes it largely inaccessible to plants. So, although there is no harm in putting the eggshells in your gardens, don't assume that eggshells alone will do much for the roses.

- If you hold a banana by the stem and pull the peel down from the bottom of the fruit the stringy parts will stay on the skin instead of on the fruit. People tend to not enjoy eating the strings, but your plants don't mind them at all.

Although coffee grounds and banana peels are great components for a home-compost bin, they contain no special capabilities when it comes to roses.

26. Rhododendrons need to be deadheaded for better blooming next season.

Remember the old quote about housework expanding to fill the time available? The same could be said about deadheading. We'd all appreciate a team of elves who would arrive in the night and remove spent blooms. Since this isn't likely, we must focus our deadheading efforts on producing the greatest results in appearance and flowering.

Most rhododendrons produce new growth while they're in full bloom, and at the end of each of those new shoots is the germ of next year's flower. Once this season's blossoms have faded, the buds that will produce flowers in eleven months are already formed. Although pruning can stimulate new growth, merely snipping off the seedpods doesn't usually produce new shoots in the current year.

> Deadheading might actually produce fewer flowers instead of more.

Many rhododendrons already have the new growth, with the germ of next year's flowers, when the current blooms are fresh.

Nonetheless, since deadheading removes developing seeds this can prompt more reliable bloom *in some species* of rhododendron.

Certain rhododendron varieties naturally flower well every other year. The plant seems to put resources into large seed production one year and then takes the following season off. For such plants, removing the spent flowers before seeds are formed can stimulate better bloom the next year as the shrub tries again for seed production.

However, studies on various types of rhododendron show that some *don't* produce significantly more flowers when deadheaded. Additionally, gardeners occasionally find that deadheading adversely affects future flowering because the tender, new growth can be inadvertently broken off. So unless we're really careful, deadheading might actually produce fewer flowers instead of more.

If you don't like how the old rhododendron flowers look, or suspect that you have a plant that takes every other year off, by all means deadhead away. But if you're short of time let Mother Nature handle this bit of housekeeping.

27. Deadhead roses by cutting down to the first set of five leaflets.

The children's television series *Sesame Street* debuted in the 1960s and began teaching number skills using fast-paced, colorful graphics. Around that time gardening books and articles started mentioning the importance of counting leaflets when deadheading roses. Coincidence? You decide.

> Remember these three words: clip, don't count.

Gardeners have been told that when clipping off wilted roses we should make the cut above a set of five leaflets. Although I'm joking when I connect this practice and the TV program, for many of us deadheading roses has felt like an episode of *Sesame Street*. "1-2-3, 1-2-3," our minds sing as we look at the plants, searching for the right place to cut. "1-2-3-4-5!"

I found one rose book that even advises to cut back to just above the *second* set of five leaflets. More counting. And then there are the articles that add geometry into our calculations as we're told to make the cut at a 45-degree angle.

Enough rose arithmetic…counting leaflets is time consuming. Fortunately, we can leave this horticultural busywork behind us. Many rose experts around the world have tested the practice of cutting "above a set of five" and found it to be completely unwarranted. They see that roses will bloom just as well, and sometimes *better*, when deadheaded by cutting just below the spent flower.

When it comes to deadheading roses, remember these three words: clip, don't count.

For some roses deadheading stimulates the production of new flowers. Others continue to bloom without deadheading or don't flower again, clipping or not.

28. You should always stake a newly planted tree.

It's admirable that we want to help our plants but sometimes we go a bit overboard. OK, *often* we go a bit overboard, a quality that must be programmed in our DNA. Consider these instructions from T.E.G., a farmer from Ohio writing in *The Bolivar bulletin* from Hardeman County, Tennessee, in 1872.

"Procure three stakes for each tree of any lasting wood," he begins clearly enough, "and of sufficient length to reach three or four inches above the connection of the main branches with the stock after having been driven or otherwise firmly placed in the ground firmly."

"Take a piece of leather (scraps of harness leather will answer the purpose very well, and will last as long as a tree requires stays) two or three inches wide, and long enough to encircle a tree that is three or four inches in diameter, close to and below the limbs," he continues. "Puncture each end of the leather in three or four places so as to admit a strong lace."

Perhaps this was clearer to readers in the late 1800s. Skipping over the rest of the detailed instructions, including the descriptions of putting

> When it comes to supporting our trees, less is more.

a stake in the southwest, east, and northwest, we'll go right to the purpose of T.E.G.'s tutorial. "No one need apprehend danger to their young trees from even terrific storms when thus secured."

Storm or no storm, T.E.G.'s trees were staked so securely that they were not going anywhere. Unfortunately, if he left such tight staking on for long they were also not going to develop a strong trunk or root system. Trees are a complex system and their growth is connected and responsive to the environment. Simply put, when it comes to root and stem growth, the action of a trunk and canopy swaying in the wind makes a plant grow stronger.

Should a newly planted tree be staked? If the canopy is so large that you're worried that it will topple or shift the tree, by all means provide some support. But don't make that support too rigid and be sure and remove it after one growing season has passed. Many a tree has been girdled to death because the staking has become an invisible part of the landscape.

When it comes to helping to supporting our trees, less is more.

A young tree with a small canopy, such as this pink-flowering 'Satomi' Kousa dogwood, doesn't need staking. In fact, allowing the trunk to move in the wind will help this plant grow a strong root system.

You can leave the burlap around the roots of a balled and burlaped shrub or tree.

A few years ago I was at a doctor's office, and as we finished up he asked, "Would you take a look at the dying shrub next to the driveway? I think it might have a disease." Pleased that the doc was asking me for a diagnosis, I went outside to examine the plant.

As soon as my eyes hit the soil line I knew what had killed this rhododendron. Although the plant had been in the ground for a few years, the remains of the burlap that had originally encased the root ball were clearly visible. The fabric was slightly decayed and rotting on the soil's surface, but the burlap was still in place underground and there was twine and burlap tightly tied around the trunk.

> "Putting anything between the tree roots and the soil is a bad idea."

Both wire baskets and burlap wrapping can cause the death of plants years later, when the plants are finally getting large and beautiful. An ounce of prevention, the removal of the burlap and wire, pays off for the future.

"Putting anything between tree roots and the soil is a bad idea," explains Scott Aker, Head of Horticulture at the U.S. National Arboretum.

"At one time, burlap was an all-natural material that decayed rapidly in soil, but today's burlap is generally treated to retard decay. This becomes a barrier to roots much longer than old-fashioned burlap ever did."

The rhododendron at my doctor's office proved to have roots that circled around and around inside the burlap, choking the stem just below the surface of the soil. Just above ground level, the twine had also strangled the trunk. Double jeopardy!

A tree or shrub can be placed in the hole with the wrapping still in place, but these should either be removed completely or flattened down to the bottom of the hole.

As for my diagnosis of my doctor's ailing plant, I told him that his shrub had died from RBD: residual burlap disorder.

30. Trees need "deep-root" feeding.

When I was young, my father would make an annual trip into our yard where several large maple trees grew. He'd be carrying a long, iron pipe, a sledgehammer, the hose, and a bag of 10-10-10 fertilizer. When he was about eight feet from a tree he'd stop and bang that pipe down three feet into the ground. Then he'd rotate the pipe to enlarge the hole, and then pull it from the earth.

Next Dad dumped a cup of fertilizer into the hole he'd made and filled it several times with water from the hose. After that, he'd move about six feet to the side and do this all over again, working in a circle around each tree. My father was deep-root feeding our maples.

Unfortunately, he was also getting a sore arm from all that pounding, and putting nitrogen and phosphorous into the water table for nothing. My father thought he was helping, but because he was putting fertilizer well below the plants' feeder roots he was just wasting his Saturday morning.

Most trees don't have roots that grow very deeply; a tree's root system is more like a

> For most trees, the top foot of soil is where the action is.

pancake than the reflection of the branching up above. After all, the top foot of soil is where the action is, so that's where the roots are concentrated. That's where decomposing leaves and other organic matter are improving the soil. That's where moisture collects and microorganisms flourish.

Many tree experts would have told my father that he shouldn't be fertilizing his trees at all. Studies show that trees do best when they are only given their own decaying foliage.

Usually it's important to remember that Mother Nature knows best and grows best.

Since people assume that tree roots grow deeply into the soil they often want to "help" where assistance isn't needed. Most tree roots grow near the surface, so we don't need to deep-root feed, nor do we need to cover roots like these that show above the soil.

31. A large crop of acorns foretells a long, cold winter.

If it were true that a bumper crop of acorns was produced before a hard winter, it would mean that oak trees were both clairvoyant and the most generous plants on earth. To provide food for animals in advance of a long winter would be uniquely magnanimous. It would also be completely contrary to how plants actually operate.

Plants have one mission on this planet: they are all about pushing their own genetics into the future. Oak trees don't care about the squirrels, birds and other wildlife that eat their nuts, though they sometimes benefit from the fact that some of these critters help disperse and bury the acorns. Oaks make acorns to grow into new oak trees, not to feed wildlife.

Why does the production of nuts change from year to year? Anyone who has oak trees has experienced times when the streets and driveways are carpeted with acorns. Not only is this overabundance messy and sometimes dangerous, but it guarantees that the following spring we'll be pulling young oak seedlings out of our gardens.

> Such discrepancies in nut growth are a satiation strategy.

While variances in acorn production can sometimes be related to weather, such discrepancies in nut growth are a satiation strategy. It's part of the plants' ultimate mission to make sure that oak trees grow in the future.

Acorns are eaten by an enormous number of animals. Birds, deer, bears, squirrels and mice are just a few of the critters that depend on these nuts. If the crop of acorns was fairly constant from year to year it would steadily sustain the population of wildlife, but not many acorns would be left to fulfill their destinies and become trees.

An occasional season of fewer acorns means that some of the wildlife depending on this nut will die because their food isn't as abundant. Follow that lean year with a bumper crop of acorns and it's almost certain that there will be many nuts that aren't eaten. In the seasons when copious acorns are produced, many more are likely to germinate and grow into new oak trees.

Mighty oaks from little acorns grow, the saying goes. In producing occasional bumper crops of nuts, oak trees are just increasing the odds that this remains true.

Many species of animals depend on acorns as food. People often view them as a nuisance, but for oak trees they are strictly for growing new oaks. Bumper crops of acorns are the plants' way of safeguarding the germination of future trees.

Did You Know...

- White oaks produce acorns in one year but the nuts on black and red oaks take two full years to mature.

- An oak tree has a juvenile period of about 20 years during which time it doesn't produce acorns. Many oaks don't make a large crop of nuts until they are around 50 years old.

- An average 100-year-old oak produces about 2,200 acorns per season, but only one acorn in 10,000 will become a tree.

- The "Live Oak" (Quercus virginiana) got its common name because it keeps its leaves in the wintertime while other oak trees are deciduous.

32. We have to coat or seal wounds on trees.

I'm convinced that our desire to paint and patch tree wounds comes from the part of us that loves our plants and wants to help them. When a tree loses a limb our instant response is cover the wound. Our plant has a boo-boo, so we rush to get out the bandages.

For years we've applied paint or tar products on recently damaged trees, but we haven't stopped there. I've seen places where well meaning homeowners have stapled aluminum foil or cardboard on such wounds. I've even seen elastic bandages.

> It seems that anything that's placed on a tree does more harm than good.

Scott Aker, Head of Horticulture at the U.S. National Arboretum, believes that people don't understand a fundamental aspect of trees. "I think the practice of sealing wounds on trees with tar or paint comes from the belief that trees are permanent and static elements in landscapes," he says. In other words, we think of trees as being similar to buildings.

"At one time, it was common to repair trees as if they were structures by filling in cavities with cement and painting over wounds," Aker continues. "Decades of these practices ended when the trees provided the proof that doing these kinds of repairs promotes more wood decay than leaving the wounds alone."

It seems that anything that's placed on a tree does more harm than good. Aker explains: "Paint and tar lock in moisture, creating a more favorable environment for decay organisms. Paint and tar also retard the growth of cambium around the outer edges of a wound, delaying the natural healing process. It's the tree's ability to grow continuously throughout its life that enables it to recover from wounds."

You can certainly assist a stressed tree by watering it deeply every couple of weeks in times of drought. But leave the bandages in the medicine cabinet.

Trees are designed to heal on their own. The best thing that people can do when a branch breaks is to make a clean cut in the "branch collar," about an inch out from the trunk of the tree.

33. The light green "moss" on the limbs of trees causes the tree to decline.

"Is that mossy stuff killing my trees?" This question is posed to arborists, garden center workers and gardening radio hosts the world round. The "mossy stuff" that is causing concern is lichen. It's frequently most noticeable in spring and fall when the host plant's leaves are thinner, and rain or mist causes the lichen to swell.

Lichen is actually a partnership between a fungus and an alga or cyanobacteria. Simply stated, the fungus provides the structure and the alga or cyanobacteria photosynthesize to produce simple sugars. Lichens are epiphytes, not parasites; they don't take any energy from the plants that they are growing on.

In addition to lichen, orchids, bromeliads, and members of the genus *Tillandsia*,

> Instead of worrying about lichen, address the conditions that are stressing the host plant.

aka "air plants," are also epiphytes. All of these get their nutrients from rainfall, dust and small amounts of decomposing debris, not from the plant they are using for support.

So why do people see more lichen on plants that are failing? Knowing that lichens photosynthesize is the key to answering this question. When a tree or shrub is weakened by stresses such as insect attack, drought or other environmental conditions, they will lose leaves. The resulting thinner canopy allows more light to reach the lichen, which promotes greater photosynthesis and growth.

Instead of worrying about lichen, address the conditions that are stressing the host plant. You might even find yourself liking lichen.

Lichen can be many colors including black, green, gray, white or yellow. It might appear almost flat against bark, or fuzzy and three-dimensional. Whether the lichen is sparse or thick, it doesn't harm the host tree.

Did you know...

- Lichens, which have antibacterial properties, have been used medicinally for over 1600 years to cover skin wounds or treat internal infections.
- Throughout the world, lichens have been used to create colorful dyes for fabrics and yarns.

34. When transplanting a shrub or tree you should cut it back substantially first.

Imagine a city that has a well-planned emergency response system in place. There are communication procedures so that in the event of a catastrophe they can immediately begin damage repair. Now envision that an outside agency, being ignorant of those emergency arrangements, sees a storm approaching the area and decides to help.

"This city won't be able to sustain all of these utilities and structures after the storm," this independent organization declares, "so we'll help them out by removing a third of it. That way they'll have less to maintain and worry about when repairs are underway."

So, with good intentions this outside agency ignorantly shuts down the very mechanisms that power the city's emergency communications. After the storm, the area's disaster response structure no longer works and the recovery takes much longer.

When it comes to transplanting shrubs and trees, our plants are that city and we humans are the outside agency. We've noticed that when a plant has had its roots cut it responds by shedding foliage. We've seen that immediately after transplantation a plant drops the leaves it can no longer support. So people have decided to assist with that process by cutting plants back *before* moving them. Unfortunately, by doing so we're disrupting that plant's communication system and thereby delaying the recovery process.

What people failed to notice is that when roots are cut plants don't jettison the growth at the *ends* of branches. In response to transplantation, plants shed their *interior* foliage. This is because there is a complex transmission system between the growing tips of plants and the root structure.

We don't need to understand the complexities of plant hormones or their growth and repair pathways. For home landscapers it's sufficient to remember these basics when transplanting shrubs and trees: 1. Dig as large a root ball as possible. 2. Don't cut the plant back before or after moving it; let the plant drop what it can no longer support. 3. Water the plant in well, immediately after transplantation and regularly afterwards. And be sure to water the area around

> In response to transplantation, plants shed their interior foliage.

the hole where the shrub or tree has been placed so that the roots have moist soil to grow into.

4. Remove deadwood at any time.

5. A year or two after transplanting, prune lightly to remove crossed branches or weak growth, and to improve appearance.

When I transplanted this Summer Wine ninebark (Physocarpus opulifolius 'Seward') I tied the branches together instead of cutting it back. This made the handling easier. After two years in its new location, the plant got reestablished and some older canes could be pruned down low in order to stimulate new growth.

35. Rusty nails make hydrangeas turn blue.

*N*ovelists positively love the idea that rusty nails make hydrangea flowers turn blue. In dozens of novels, fictional characters pound oxidized spikes around plants with hammers, add them to watering cans or throw them into planting holes. It's the kind of small detail that gives invented individuals depth, veracity and color…literally. You can picture the reddish rust of the nails and the sky-blue hydrangeas.

> The connection between rusty nails and flower color borders on fiction itself.

Unfortunately, the connection between rusty nails and flower color borders on fiction itself.

Yes, many *Hydrangea macrophylla* (and subspecies *serrata*) will change flower color from pink to blue because of metal in the soil. But the element responsible is actually aluminum. If the soil is acidic, the shrub can absorb aluminum from the soil and the flowers will be blue. If the pH of the ground is alkaline, the aluminum can't be absorbed and the blossoms will be pink.

Fiction aside, I've found many references to the rusty nails myth where people swear that this trick turned their hydrangea flowers blue. My guess is that because the nails used were high in iron sulfate, and this chemical compound is one way of acidifying soil, this is the reason some saw results with this practice. The nails probably helped swing the pH of the soil in the acidic direction.

The oddest recommendation I've seen was to use "rusty aluminum nails." This is really nonsensical because nails made of aluminum don't rust. I suspect that the author of this variation knew

To be able to pick a bouquet of hydrangea flowers in September makes a person feel wealthy indeed. In this bouquet, several varieties of the white-flowering pee-gee hydrangea (Hydrangea paniculata) show the pink hues that develop in late summer or fall. Even though these flowers change from white to pink, nothing will turn them blue.

that aluminum was the key to being blue, and was trying to combine the myth with reality.

When working with hydrangea color, start by testing pH of your soil. It's helpful to first know the dirt's natural acidity or alkalinity so you can adjust from there. If you desire blue hydrangeas you can use aluminum sulfate, which adds aluminum and acidifies the soil. Be sure to use this product according to directions, however, as too much will damage the plant. Excess aluminum will turn some hydrangeas a false looking swimming pool turquoise.

Applying sulfur is another way to make soil acidic. And if blue isn't your color, hydrangeas can be turned or kept pink by adding lime around the plants in spring and fall.

White hydrangeas always stay white although most varieties of H. paniculata will develop a blush of pink in the fall as the flowers age. The only way to turn a white hydrangea blue is with spray paint…or if you're writing fiction.

Big leaf, or mophead, hydrangeas (Hydrangea macrophylla) can have blue and pink flowers on them at the same time. In this case the plant is growing near concrete, which makes some sections of the soil more alkaline than others. The combination of mixed alkaline and acidic patches of ground produces an assortment of hues on this plant.

36. You can't grow a female holly without a male holly close by.

"Birds do it, bees do it," begins Cole Porter's song. Although this songwriter didn't include them in his lyrics, our plants are going at it all the time. Yes, plants have a sex life and the flowers are usually where the action is. Most

> The only reason to have both male and female plants is so that the females will have berries.

plants have bisexual blooms, that is, flowers with both female and male parts. But like human sexuality, some plants' reproductive processes are wide-ranging and occasionally complicated.

These two female American holly (Ilex opaca) are kept well-berried by the male tree that grows nearby. Female trees would still grow without the male, but wouldn't produce the fruit that makes birds and gardeners happy.

A few plants have separate flowers that are either male or female, all blooming on the same plant. There are usually enough of each gender for pollination and seed production but random plants can make flowers of only one sex. Remember that zucchini you grew that only produced male flowers and never developed squash?

Avocado trees have flowers that change their sex daily. One group of trees have flowers that open as females in the morning only to close and reopen with male parts in the afternoon. The second group of avocados does this in reverse making it advisable for those who want fruit to plant one of each type. Yes, this sounds just far-fetched enough to be a garden myth. Sometimes truth *is* stranger than fiction.

Not all hollies can be called "bushes-with-benefits" but many in this genus are either male or female. Although it's romantic to think that every shrub needs a mate, in reality you could plant all male holly or all females and they'd grow just fine. The only reason to have both male and female plants is so that the females will have berries. Without the male's pollen the female's flowers will just shrivel instead of forming fruit.

Gardeners looking for specific results like avocados or bright red holly berries need to be matchmakers and provide the right plant types or combination of sexes. But if you don't want fruit it isn't necessary to play cupid.

Did You Know...

Interesting facts about the birds and the bees:

- Did you know why so many fragrant flowers are white? Such plants are using fragrance to lure in night-flying insects for pollination. White blossoms are more obvious landing pads in the dark.

- Over 20,000 species of plants use vibrators as part of their sex lives: their flowers are buzz-pollinated. These plants hold their pollen in a way that only the vibrations from bees or a few other insects will release it. Bumblebees cling onto these plants and buzz at frequencies that release a cloud of pollen onto the vibrating insect. Although most of this pollen is used for food, some of it is transported from flower to flower, pollinating the plants.

- Some flowers are marked like airport landing strips. Those dark splotches against a light background on foxglove flowers and the streaks of yellow on some iris petals are like arrows painted on a runway. The flowers' markings are telling their pollinators to "Land here! This way in!"

- Plants that are pollinated by wind instead of insects tend to have small, green flowers that aren't scented. Since they depend on the breezes to spread their pollen, there is no reason to attract insects with color or fragrance. Such plants also produce lots of pollen that is very lightweight. The perfect example of this is ragweed. People blame goldenrod for their ragweed allergies because these plants bloom at the same time and the goldenrod has showy, yellow flowers. But it is the insignificant, almost invisible ragweed bloom that is responsible for our suffering.

37. When looking for screening, plant a row of the fastest growing shrubs or trees you can find.

We live in a fast food, instant coffee, high-speed Internet culture. So it's no wonder that we want our landscaping to be immediate as well. Every nursery worker frequently hears the following comment: "I need a privacy screen. What's the fastest growing evergreen?"

It's understandable that people don't want to wait years and years for a secluded environment, but a line of plants that grow quickly might not be the best choice. Although the screen will develop rapidly, the shrubs or trees that create the barrier keep growing. Many people have found themselves being crowded off their property by their screening. It's not possible to tell a Leyland cypress or Green Giant arborvitae, "OK, you can stop growing now."

There are additional reasons that a row of one fast growing plant isn't the best choice for privacy. If you've planted a row of all one type of plant, and an insect or disease comes along that attacks that variety, you could lose your entire screening. New insect pests and other problems

> When it comes to a privacy screen, consider using a mix of plants.

travel the globe and regularly pop up in new areas. Since most pests target specific plants, the homeowner who plants just one type of screening is vulnerable.

It's not unusual for environmental conditions to destroy plants, and this is also problematic for those who've planted a single kind of shrub or tree. If the screen has grown large, and one or more plants are damaged or killed by wind, snow or other situations, it will be difficult to find a sizeable plant as a replacement. A damaged screen that's only one type of plant will always look marred.

When it comes to a privacy screen, consider using a mix of plants. Place one or more fast growing shrubs or trees where you need the most coverage. Then add other varieties, some single plants and others in groups of three or five, on both sides of those chosen for rapid growth. If you also choose plants with different foliage colors and textures or bloom times, you'll have a more interesting, colorful screen.

Perhaps a planting for privacy shouldn't be all or nothing.

Not everyone can grow camellias like this beauty at Polly Hill Arboretum on Martha's Vineyard, but a mix of different evergreen plants for screening can be emulated by all.

38. Plant *Clematis* with their heads in the sun and their feet in the shade.

There's nothing like a good slogan. *Winston tastes good like a cigarette should. M&M's melt in your mouth, not in your hand. Got milk?* Each of us could rattle off several such phrases that are stuck in our brains, like it or not.

When an idea is well phrased, it's memorable, and the *Clematis* vine has had just such a slogan for years. The majority of gardeners can tell you that *Clematis* like "their heads in the sun and their feet in the shade." I've found references to that exact wording in print going back to the early 1920s. Although it's a saying that clearly has sticking power, it's not really true.

There are large, wholesale *Clematis* growers all over the world who raise these vines in black plastic pots, often on ground covered with back landscape fabric, in full sun. There are home-owners who, ignorant of the vine's jingle, plant a solo *Clematis* on the lamppost in dead-on sunshine. Given adequate water, the plants in both situations thrive.

Which brings us to how this myth was generated. *Clematis* grows best with a fairly consistent level of moisture. So in the days before irrigation

> *Clematis* will be perfectly happy with sunny feet.

was common, it made sense to shade the area around the roots in order to preserve moisture. Mulch is the best for this purpose; other plants not only shade the area but also compete with the *Clematis* for available water.

A diamond is forever, Frosted Flakes are Grrreat! and as long as you don't let them get completely dry, *Clematis* will be perfectly happy with sunny feet.

'Nelly Moser' is one variety of Clematis *that flowers reliably in part-shade.*

Compost,
Soils, Mulch
&
Fertilizers

"The best fertilizer is a gardener's shadow."
– Author unknown

39. Oak leaves and pine needles make compost or soil more acidic.

Some years ago I gave a talk titled, "Myths, Lies and All The Latest Dirt," to a convention of volunteer master gardeners in upstate New York. I spoke about many of the common gardening myths, including the belief that oak leaves and pine needles can affect soil acidity.

> **Many areas with oak and pine forests have naturally acidic soils.**

Just because oaks and pines flourish in areas where the soil is acidic doesn't mean that their leaves and needles caused the acidity.

After the talk I was walking to the plant sale when one of the master gardeners approached. "I enjoyed your talk," she began, although I noticed she looked annoyed. "Except I don't agree with one thing you said. Pine needles and oak leaves do make soil acidic." Her stance alone told me she was willing to fight me on this one, should I be ready to "take it outside."

This myth is very deeply entrenched in the public's consciousness. It has been so often published in gardening books and repeated from person to person that it's as ingrained in our belief system as the certainty of death and taxes. But while demise is inevitable, and taxes are a pretty sure thing, pine needles, oak leaves and coffee grounds don't make soil or compost acidic.

Although pine needles and oak leaves might have a low pH in their raw, pre-compost form, once they have decomposed they are closer to neutral – and no, that isn't because their acid is leached into the ground. In the composting process pH is neutralized; test any finished compost and it will come in at around 6.5, whether it's been made from oak leaves, pine needles, coffee grounds or other materials.

There have been voices of dissent who've tried to spread this word for years. I found a mention of this lore in The *Ohio Conservation Bulletin* from 1948. "Contrary to popular belief, oak leaves, pine needles, moss, weathered sawdust and rotted apple pumice will not acidify the soil," the author wrote.

So why does this myth linger? Perhaps it's because many areas with oak and pine forests have naturally acidic soils. This stems from the minerals in the soil, not the trees that grow there.

If you want to mulch your acid-loving rhododendrons with pine needles or oak leaves, I'm sure they'll be quite happy. Your alkaline lovers, such as lilacs, will love the same treatment, however, and the compost made from these materials can be spread on any garden.

Death and taxes? A sure thing. Pine trees, oak leaves and soil acidity? Not so much…although I have no interest in fighting about it.

Pine needles can be used to mulch vegetable gardens without fear that they will make soil acidic.

40. Mulch robs the soil of nitrogen.

"Slick Willie" Sutton had a forty-year criminal career robbing banks. He captured the public's imagination because he wore many disguises and never carried a loaded gun because, he said, somebody might get hurt. He was a likeable offender who took from the rich and kept what he stole. Some people think of mulch as being the Slick Willie of the garden: pleasant, adaptable, and an out-and-out thief.

> A thin layer of mulch on the surface won't take nutrients from the soil.

It is true that most mulches are high in carbon, and such materials use nitrogen as they break down. This is why composters aim for a mix of high-carbon and high-nitrogen substances in their compost bins. By piling nitrogen-rich grass clippings or fresh kitchen scraps into a pile of dried leaves and wood clippings, the microbes that break down plant matter are kept well fed and compost is the result.

Those same microbes are at work in our gardens, composting fallen plant debris as well as the mulch we put down. They work at the place where mulch meets the soil and they need nitrogen to live, so at that place there might be a slight reduction in nitrogen in the soil. Given a soil that has plenty of nitrogen in the first place, as long as the high-carbon mulch isn't turned into the soil there will be plenty of nitrogen down below for plants.

Mulch is slick for the garden in many ways, most notably for weed control, moisture retention and soil amendment. Wood mulches such as chips and bark mulch are good for all three and are available in most regions. Used

Many choose bark mulch for weed and moisture control around shrubs and perennials. As long as the mulch isn't too thick, and it isn't turned into the soil, this covering functions well, adds organic matter to the soil, and doesn't take nutrients away from plants.

on ornamental beds where the soil isn't turned, they'll be functional for your garden without turning to a life of crime.

Mulching and Your Gardens

Do all gardens need to be mulched? Absolutely not. Although in many neighborhoods a mulched bed is the norm, not the exception, it's an optional practice. You might want to avoid mulch if your soil tends to be wet, as it will keep even more water in the ground. Vegetable gardeners who turn the soil with tillers or a hoe for weed control might find mulches more of a problem than a benefit. Finally, some people just prefer the look of bare soil or plants that are growing so thickly that there isn't room for a mulch cover anyway.

In this time, when everyone is increasingly concerned about sustainability, gardeners and home landscapers wonder how responsible it is to purchase mulches that are shipped long distances before they're used. For those who are more comfortable sourcing their mulching materials locally, consider using chopped leaves or chipped wood.

Many homeowners can chop leaves in the fall using their lawnmower and apply those around shrubs, trees and perennials as mulch. These can also be piled in the fall and used in a thin layer on vegetable and annual beds. Local arborists and landscapers are often willing to sell or dump

This plant-lover's garden was mulched with an attractive layer of chopped oak leaves. Many people already have an abundance of leaves on their properties; doesn't it make sense to use what's already there whenever possible?

chipped branches and trees when requested. Some mulches may be locally available as a result of regional agriculture – like peanut hulls, nutshells, hops, and pine needles.

Two organic materials that should be avoided for mulching are sawdust and peat moss. Both of these form such a solid sheet on the surface of the soil that it will repel water.

41. Cedar mulch keeps insects out of the garden.

I graduated from high school in a time when local stores presented every senior girl with a small cedar chest made by the Lane Furniture Company. The gift was a gentle reminder to the girls and their parents that they might want to invest in the larger hope or blanket chest. Such cedar trunks were used to hold woolens and household linens, keeping them safe from moths. The mini-chest gifts were eventually discontinued because the times, and the fibers used to make blankets and clothing, they were a-changin'.

People still associate cedar with insect control. It seems that cedar storage for moth protection worked because the odor of the wood's oils covered the scent of the wool. Moths were therefore less likely to find the woolens and lay their eggs there. You can still purchase cedar hangers, oil and cedar chests, but there is only anecdotal evidence that the wood has true insecticidal qualities in the closet.

Gardeners often bring this cedar chest mentality into their landscapes, where there is no repellant benefit at all. Outdoors, the bugs treat cedar as they do any other shredded wood.

Cedar mulch does not keep insects away from your plants, yard or dwelling.

> Cedar mulch does not keep insects away from your plants, yard or dwelling.

The choice of which mulch to use should be made based on aesthetics, practicality and budget. Choose the organic material you like best. Heavier mulches stay in place better in windy areas or on slopes, so in these situations a gardener might choose a heftier shredded bark over, say, lightweight cocoa hulls.

When using mulch for moisture retention and weed suppression, choose a finer material instead of large chunks. Smaller pieces create a denser covering that will hold more water in the soil and prevent light from triggering the germination of weed seeds. If cost is the determining factor, using leaves and/or pine needles that have fallen on your property is an inexpensive and sustainable approach. Use a lawn mower to chop the leaves before spreading them in your gardens; smaller pieces stay in place better, suppress weeds more efficiently, and look more attractive. (By the way, I still have my little Lane chest. There it is, looking hopeful, sitting in a cedar-mulched herb garden.)

I still have the Lane mini-chest that was given to me when I graduated from high school. Unfortunately, the safety we associate with cedar chests can't be taken into the garden. The cedar mulch used on this herb garden is attractive, has a pleasant odor, and like all organic mulches it amends soil from the top down. It does not discourage the insects.

42. Amend soil with equal parts manure, peat moss, and soil when you plant a tree or shrub.

The first trees I ever planted were put in according to the standard recommendations at that time. Everyone knew the formula: a third native soil, a third manure, and a third peat moss. Because we'd been told "Dig a five-dollar hole for a fifty-cent tree" we dutifully excavated large spaces for planting. After mixing those three ingredients together we planted our trees, filling hole around the roots with our improved soil. Twenty years later, I returned to that property and saw one reason why this is no longer the recommended way to plant.

The trees, two living and one dead, were now in depressions. They were growing out of bowls. The two that were still alive were fortunate that their bowls were on a slope that drained on the downhill side. The dead tree wasn't as lucky; its bowl retained water, since the native soil was heavy clay. Why were these trees now in a depression? Because the peat and manure had decomposed over time.

In addition to the decomposition of organic amendments in a planting hole, studies have shown that there are other reasons not to amend soil in small areas. It turns out that enriching the soil in a planting hole can create reduced root systems; the plant doesn't want to leave the five star restaurant to go to the fast food joint next door.

> Enriching the soil in a planting hole can create reduced root systems.

Instead of that five-dollar hole, gardeners and landscapers are now advised to dig a five-dollar bowl that spreads wide but is only as deep as the root ball being planted. The native soil that was taken out is then replaced around the new plant. Since the hole was wide, there is an area of loosened dirt that roots can grow into quickly.

As for amendments such as compost or manure, these should be applied on top of the soil in a wide area around the plant. Again, we are well served to copy how nature amends soil – from the top down.

If perennial, annual and vegetable beds are to be improved with compost or manure, it's best to mix those organics into the entire bed, not just the planting hole. The top-down amendment method can then be used on established or previously enriched beds.

Looking Back...

The recommendations for amending soil in the hole go way back. Here are some references to this practice I've found.

From the April 8, 1897 edition of *Ranche and range*, from North Yakima, Washington, comes this counsel:

"In planting make good-sized holes. When I planted trees 40 years ago in California I had my holes dug 2 ½ feet deep and 3 feet in diameter and mixed well rotted fertilizer with the dirt to fill the hole with; and I have since seen no reason to change that plan unless it be to make the hole bigger. Then with plenty of muscular activity and ordinary judgment the trees can be brought into bearing."

This guidance for planting makes me realize that the desire for fast results isn't unique to 21st century gardeners. R. Trimmer, writing in the *Omaha daily bee* in November of 1905 writes that manure should be freely used.

"I have observed that many people in planting don't use any manure. or very little, many of them saying they are going to use liquid manure in the summer. That is all right if that is done, but the cheapest way is to use a good deal of manure while planting. Dig the holes large enough and put manure in the bottom mixed up with the soil and put more soil on top so that the roots of the tree don't come in contact with the manure, but it ought to be in easy reach of them, so when they form new fibrous roots the manure soon can be reached by them. In our short-lived age we want quick results and I don't see any other way to get them."

When planting new gardens, the old recommendation was to have a big wheelbarrow on hand for mixing peat and manure into the native dirt. Now we know that entire beds should be amended, not individual planting holes. This entire garden was amended with composted manure. When it came time to lay the path, a layer of soil was removed and replaced with sand where large steppingstones were placed.

43. Flower beds or veggie gardens should be started by "double digging."

Some myths are buried so deeply in the collective consciousness that they persist over centuries despite all evidence to the contrary. The practice of double digging, also known as "subsoiling" or "bastard trenching," is an example of a technique so (forgive me) deeply rooted that it might take quadruple excavating to get rid of this falsehood.

In researching how long this myth has been with us, I found mention of the practice in gardening books from the late 19th and early 20th centuries. *Yard and Garden*, by Tarkington Baker, and published in 1908, was typical.

This book is subtitled *A Book of Practical Information for the Amateur Gardener in City, Town or Suburb*, and it extols the benefits of double digging. "There is no better method of preparing the soil than that which the English gardener terms 'Bastard Trenching,'" the author writes. "It is effective and not difficult to execute."

I'm thinking that Mr. Baker must have had some other poor bastard to do his digging for him. Anyone who has lifted many shovelfuls of

> No one has been double digging soil in the jungles, woods and fields... and they seem to have done quite well without it.

soil isn't likely to stress the lack of difficulty in such labors.

Double digging involves removing the soil from a bed to the depth of one shovel length, about twelve inches. This dirt is put aside on a tarp or in a wheel-barrow. In true double digging, a second foot is then removed and the first batch put into the bottom of the hole along with soil amend-ments such as manure. The second layer is also amended and placed on the top.

Bastard trenching allows that the bottom layer could be turned and amended in place, instead of removed and switched with the topsoil. The name might have been given because the process was initially seen as being inferior to the doubly dug bed where both layers were removed. In either case, however, digging a foot or two of soil out of an area is *hard work*. It's also not necessary.

The thinking has been that if the soil is loose and enriched to a depth of two feet, a plant's roots will grow deeper and faster. Unfortunately, this assumes that an idea that people have about how plants will grow best is somehow better than the way plants have actually been growing since they began. No one has been double digging soil in the jungles, woods and fields where plants have evolved and they seem to have done quite well without it.

What I found surprising is that although some older sources were extolling this process, others have been refuting it for years. For example, an issue of *The Hawaiian Gazette*, published July 16, 1915, contains the headline "Subsoiling Costs More Than Worth."

The article goes on to say that experiments by the English team of Pickering and Russell, conducted over a series of years and with a variety of soil types, demonstrated little value in this practice. The subtitles say it all: *Science Again Overthrows Old Ideas on Correct Cultivation Practise in Fields; No Real Gain* and *An Expensive Practise*.

The article, speaking specifically to those who raised sugar cane, states that no benefit in growth rates or soil moisture is gained from double digging. "Modern agricultural science teaches that top soils are the richest," it says. "The feeding roots of plants never go very deep if there is water, plant food and aeration in the surface soils."

A hundred years ago it was known that the natural soil structure is important and nature creates this perfectly, without our intervention. So why do people continue to believe that the laborious process of double digging is somehow better? Ignore those who keep this myth alive. Amend soil from the top down, like nature does it, and save time and your back.

These gardens at Poison Ivy Acres grow vegetables, berries, annuals, perennials, shrubs and trees. Clearly, a garden geek lives here. These gardens were only five years old when this photo was taken, yet none of the area was prepared by double digging.

44. Lighten clay soils by adding sand.

When my husband and I moved to Spencertown, New York, we knew we wanted a vegetable garden. We asked Albert Verenazi, our neighbor and a lifelong farmer, to level a piece of our land for this purpose. Later that week he arrived with a backhoe. Seeing Albert's truck parked on the side of the road, several local residents stopped to view what was going on. I soon found myself standing in our yard with six or seven men, watching the backhoe sculpt out our new garden.

For a while we silently observed Albert at work. Then one of the men shook his head dolefully. "Some people got the rock," he declared, "and some people got the clay. You got the rock *and* the clay."

In the eleven years we lived in the mid-Hudson Valley, we became well acquainted with both the rock and the clay. Every time we planted a shrub or tree we wished that Albert's backhoe was still on the property; digging holes in that soil was hard work. When I bought perennials with tags that read, "prefers good drainage" I'd roll my eyes and wish those plants luck. We had the rock and the clay, but what we didn't have was good drainage.

Since water flows well through sand, it might seem sensible to mix that grit into clay soils. Yet this practice actually does more harm than good. The process of incorporating sand into clay disrupts the soil structure, resulting in drainage that is actually worse then before.

Good soil structure is created over time by decaying organic matter, insects, earthworms, freezing or thawing, and the movement of water. These and a few other components make the aggregates of soil and small pockets of air that allow water to sink into the earth. Even in clay soils, water penetrates better when the natural structure is kept intact. Mixing sand into clay crushes the aggregates and squeezes out the air, resulting in poor drainage.

Mother Nature amends soil from the top down, and this is how we handled our gardens in Spencertown. Once the vegetable garden was leveled, it was amended with composted manure before mulching with hay and chopped leaves.

> Even in clay soils, water penetrates better when the natural structure is kept intact.

It took a couple of years for the structure to be restored after the use of the equipment. The perennial beds and shrub borders on the property were also mulched annually, and the insects and earthworms assisted us by pulling some of this organic matter below the soil's surface.

We planted marigolds and other annuals in all the gardens and left their roots to rot in place after the fall frost. In other words, we copied what nature was doing in surrounding woods and fields, and grew gardens that thrived in the rock and the clay.

Although this large bush clover (Lespedeza thunbergii 'Gibraltar') is known to prefer good drainage, it is thriving here in heavy clay soil. The slight slope of this bed may help, since the area is never filled with standing water. The annual Blue My Mind Evolvulus appreciates the even level of moisture that this organically amended clay soil retains.

The Pleasures of Clay

Although digging in clay is difficult, heavy soils have benefits for gardeners. Clay holds onto water and nutrients in ways that sandy soils do not. This means that plants growing in clay don't need to be fertilized as much or as frequently. Once clay soils are well saturated, the gardener doesn't have to provide as much supplemental watering.

Plants that appreciate good drainage can still thrive in clay soils, provided they're not put in areas that collect standing water. Land that slopes is perfect for such plants because they won't have "wet feet" for extended periods. For varieties that want better drainage, plant on an incline.

There are many plants that thrive in clay soils. Remember that old gardener's mantra: "right plant, right place."

Selected Plants for Clay Soil

(Note: when just the genus name is given, that indicates that there are several species and/or hybrids that would thrive in clay soils.)

Perennials

Asters (Symphyotrichum)
Black-eyed Susans (Rudbeckia)
Daylilies (Hemerocallis)
False indigo (Baptisia australis)
Ferns (most varieties)
Goldenrod (Solidago)
Hellebores (Helleborus)
Hosta (Hosta)
Iris, Siberian and Japanese (Iris)
Tickseed (Coreopsis)

Shrubs

Forsythia (Forsythia)
Hinoki false cypress (Chamaecyparis obtuse)
Hydrangea (Hydrangea)
Japanese kerria (Kerria japonica)
Lilacs (Syringa)
Redtwig dogwood (Cornus sericea)
Spiraea (Spiraea)
Viburnum (Viburnum)
Weigela (Weigela)
Yew (Taxus x media)

Trees

Riverbirch (Betula nigra)
Willows (Salix)
Crabapple (Malus)
Serviceberry (Amelanchier)

Bulbs

Camassia
Crocus
Grape hyacinths (Muscari armeniacum)
Daffodils (Narcissus)

Grasses

Maiden grass (Miscanthus sinensis)
Switch grass (Panicum virgatum)
Feather reed grass (Calamagrostis x acutiflora)

Annuals

Gomphrena
Marigolds (Tagetes erecta)

45. Soil amendments such as compost or fertilizers need to be turned into the soil.

If you can only visit one public garden in the United States, go to Chanticleer in Wayne, Pennsylvania. Their diversity of plants and the creativity with which they are combined is astonishing. Even a simple trip to the restroom causes plant lovers to hyperventilate.

> Soil in the woods and fields is amended from the top down.

One of the plantings I love most at Chanticleer is called The Serpentine. Every year, these wavy beds are filled with an agricultural crop. This is a good educational opportunity, since many who visit these gardens may be unfamiliar with plants such as tobacco or barley. This curving planting gives visitors the chance to appreciate these plants in a new way. It's also appropriate to include agricultural crops in a pleasure garden, because many of our gardening practices have their roots in agriculture.

One of those customs is the turning of soil amendments such as manure or fertilizer into the ground. Ever since farmers learned the value of adding enrichments, the practice has been to turn them under. The farming column in *The Wichita Daily Eagle* from February 4, 1898 is a good example:

"Plow or spade the ground as deep as possible, and then spread over the surface manure to the depth of two or three inches, working it well into the soil." the author advises. After giving an application rate for nitrate of soda, bone meal and muriate of potash, the author instructs that these too be turned under. *"Let it be done the first warm day; be sure and work the manure and fertilizer well into the soil, and make the soil as fine as possible. Then leave it until April, when the ground should be worked over again."*

Surface applications of soil amendments are visible in these beds of tobacco plants at Chanticleer, in Wayne, Pa. In addition to making visitors to this garden more familiar with the beauty of agricultural crops, these beds speak of the connection that ornamental gardeners have with farming.

Although farmers have long turned amendments into the soil, this doesn't mean that they have to be buried to be effective. Unless soil amendments are being placed on a slope where they might wash off in a heavy rain, there is no need to dig them into the ground. In fact, doing so around established plants can injure existing root systems.

Home gardeners become inspired and informed by many sources: farms, public gardens, and the natural world. When it comes to soil amendments, especially in established gardens, we can learn best from Mother Nature and what goes on in nature. No one is out in wild areas digging composted debris or fertilizer into the ground. Soil in the woods and fields is amended from the top down.

At Chanticleer, a different agricultural crop is grown in the Serpentine gardens every year. This year, corn was featured in these beds where the soil hasn't been turned in several years.

46. Gardens need to be fertilized every year.

There is no debate that fertilizers can do wonders for plants and gardens. But when I read recommendations for frequent fertilizing I can't help but think of shampoo. Some hair washing products recommend daily use and for years many have contained the following additional instruction: "Rinse and repeat."

> Using too much fertilizer is as foolish as applying too much shampoo.

Repeat? Really? Do people who shower regularly need to wash their hair *twice*? Even a daily shampooing isn't always the best for our curly locks. These instructions serve the shampoo company's bottom line, not hygiene or healthy heads of hair.

Using too much fertilizer is as foolish as applying too much shampoo. It not only comes with a cost for the consumer, but for our plants and regional environments as well. Although it would be great to make yard and plant care simple with one easy recommendation, fertilizing just can't be reduced to one-size-fits-all.

Soil fertility varies greatly, not only from region to region, but even from neighborhood to neighborhood or yard to yard. Even on one property it's foolish to assume that the entire landscape needs the same application of fertilizer, because some plants are heavier feeders than others.

Fertilizing doesn't have to be complicated and you don't need a special food for every type of plant you grow. But between shampooing twice daily and only bathing once a week there is a great deal of room for variance, and so it is for garden fertilization.

Just one example of a garden kept on a lean diet can be seen in this hot, roadside bed. It was filled with drought tolerant plants such as yarrow, yucca, verbascum and butterfly weed. Although the ground is amended by wood chip mulch, it has never received fertilizer because fertilized plants grow larger, needing more water.

Did You Know...
From Years Gone By

Sponge fertilizer?

Newspapers in 1913 report that the Department of Agriculture's bureau of soils was evaluating the loggerhead sponge for use as a fertilizer. An article in a 1913 issue of the *Abbeville progress* newspaper from Abbeville Parish, La., says, *"This sponge, according to Mr. Thomas E. Reedy of Key West, grows in countless thousands and to an enormous size in shallow water, where it is easy to procure. Mr. Reedy also states that farmers of the Florida keys use the loggerhead sponge with wonderful results and hardly ever use chemical fertilizers."* In 1914, the U.S. Patent Office recorded an application for a patent on a plant food made from dried, granulated loggerhead sponges, and there are records of a factory being built outside of Miami for the manufacture of loggerhead sponge fertilizers.

Homemade Fertilizer Recipe

Are the bones piling up in your house? For those do-it-yourselfers, here's an idea from *The times dispatch*, published in Richmond, Va., Feb. 9, 1913:

An Odd Fertilizer for Plants

Many persons who have houseplants and flowers in the garden which do not seem to grow and bloom as they should, wonder how some people seem to grow flowers with little apparent effort.

One of the most important secrets of success, both indoors and out, is to know what is needed for fertilizers.

In many instances it is difficult to secure soil that is not impoverished and naturally deprived of the essential elements required by nature to produce healthy foliage and brilliant and profuse bloom.

One of the easiest methods to secure the required elements to enrich ordinary soil is available to all. Take bones from meat that has not been salted, such as fowls and fresh meats from the butcher, break them into small pieces and place quite a lot in an earthen jar. Cover with a solution of strong lye.

After it has stood for a few days, stir it thoroughly, and it will become a sort of mush. If possible, add a little soot from the stove or fireplace and stir again.

Place a teaspoonful of this mixture in a gallon of water and apply this to the soil about the plants twice a week. If the plants seem to have merely existed in a poor soil, give them a little more, or the same amount oftener.

The foliage will soon brighten up and the flowers, if any, will soon show a great change. If the plants have not been blooming, they will soon begin.

Nitrogen, phosphoric acid, potash, lime and other essentials are secured from such a mixture. A little of it thoroughly incorporated in the soil of an open bed will certainly assist greatly where it is difficult to obtain the proper kinds of manure.

Soil sprinkled with water mixed as described will produce fine vegetable growths. It is possible in this way to make good use of al the bones that accumulate in a home.

47. All non-blooming plants should be given fertilizer to make them come into bloom.

At some point in your life you've probably had a hangover from consuming too much alcohol and someone has suggested a quick fix. Perhaps they recommended a large, greasy breakfast, copious amounts of coffee, glasses of water or "the hair of the dog."

None of these were the speedy cure you were looking for, right? Usually you have to let time go by and your abused body will heal.

When something is amiss there is seldom an instant, no-fail fix. Similarly, for plants that aren't blooming – there isn't one go-to remedy. If a plant isn't flowering, don't immediately assume that it needs better fertilization. There are other reasons that plants don't bloom, so go through this checklist first:

> If a plant isn't flowering, don't immediately assume that it needs better fertilization.

1. *Is this plant growing in deep shade?* Many plants that normally flower won't do so if they aren't getting enough sunlight. Be aware that over time our properties change, and areas that once were in full sun might now be reduced to an hour or less per day as plants grow larger and create more shade. Watch the area where your non-blooming plant is located and get an accurate count on the hours of direct sunlight the area receives.

2. *Is your plant relatively new in your landscape and if so, was it a balled-and-burlaped plant when you bought it?* Shrubs and trees that are B&B have had the majority of their roots cut off. Depending on the variety and the size of the plant, these can take five or more years to recover from that trauma. If your plant is new and you

This small, variegated dogwood (Cornus kousa 'Wolf Eyes') grew for several years in my gardens before it started to flower. All plants have a non-flowering juvenile period; the small dogwood just wasn't old enough. The first year this tree blossomed there was just one bloom.

suspect that it had its root system pruned significantly, know that the plant's energies are being directed underground. Help it to recover with deep, weekly soakings, but forgo the fertilizer for a while.

3. *What is the pH of your soil, and is it appropriate for the plant that's not flowering?* Some plants are picky about how acid or alkaline the soil is, and we humans often make assumptions about the pH without having the soil tested. Have the dirt around a non-flowering plant tested for pH. Better yet, have a complete soil test done so that you know if nutrients are truly the reason the plant doesn't bloom.

4. *Is the plant old enough to flower?* There is a juvenile period during which plants cannot bloom. For trees, this is usually a matter of several years. No amount of fertilizer will help a young plant that's still in its juvenile period to come into flower.

5. *Is your plant known to be a heavy feeder that flowers on new growth?* Roses and many of the new annuals fall into this category and require a higher rate of fertilization. Conversely, some plants bloom better in infertile soil or when under stress. Before automatically reaching for the plant food, find out what growing conditions your particular selections need for flowering.

The phrase "Too much of a good thing" is a cliché because it's so true. An excess of food or drink, be it pastries, alcohol or plant fertilizer, isn't usually in our best interest.

Let's drink to that!

The wisteria that Gordon Gaskill originally planted in this Provincetown garden has clearly been in bloom, evidenced by the prolific seedpods. For many years, however, this plant didn't flower. Although it was probably just age that eventually brought this vine into bloom, Gordon insisted that threats helped.

48. When planting, push the soil in very firmly.

Often, plants succeed against all odds. Thank goodness that's true, because we humans do some pretty wacky things in the landscape and with our houseplants. One of those zany practices is our continued insistence on packing the soil firmly around seeds and roots. If plants could talk, many of them would be yelling, "I can't take all of this pressure!"

As a newbie gardener, I was told to stomp hard on the ground when planting trees and shrubs. This wasn't unique to the late 20th century, either. Throughout the 1880s, many small town papers ran the following recommendation in their farm and garden columns:

Peter Henderson says, in the *Prairie Farmer*: *"If garden seeds, when planted in the spring, are firmly pressed when under the earth, by the ball of the foot at the time the gardeners are putting them into the ground, they will invariably grow, drought or no drought; and, what is still more important, they will spring up earlier and grow faster, and mature better than any of their kind which have not be subjected to this discipline. This same rule of pressure holds good in transplanting trees, shrubs, and plants."*

> Small air spaces are important to good soil structure.

Pressing firmly with the feet wasn't enough pressure for some gardeners. In the early 1900s, several publications repeated the following suggestion, attributed to original publication in *The Chicago Tribune*. "Spencer U. Pickering, with his recent researches, declares that proper tree planting means a small hole, roots doubled up anyhow, the trees stuck in, the soil thrown in and rammed down as for a gate post."

Rammed down as for a gate-post? Yikes. The article then continues, *"By whatever criterion the trees are gauged the new method is said to give better results than the orthodox. Although an antagonistic cry has been raised against the revolution [sic] theory no practical man has been able to give any reason for the old faith that is in him beyond the fact that it is sanctioned by established custom."*

I can think of several reasons to avoid ramming and go back to "the old faith," beginning with the fact that the gate post doesn't have roots that are expected to grow into soil that's had the air forced out of it.

Not only do plants have a hard time pushing roots into compacted soil, but water can't run

through such ground as easily, either. Small air spaces are important to good soil structure. Nature creates these pockets in undisturbed soils when roots die and rot, earthworms and insects tunnel through the ground, and organic matter decomposes. Can you picture Mother Nature stomping around the woods and fields with heavy boots? Me neither.

It's true that we want our seeds to make good contact with the soil. Seeds are better able to germinate when they touch moist earth. And we don't want huge pockets of air next to newly placed plant roots because these might cause the roots to shrivel and die.

A gentle pat to push seeds into place, and a slight push to the soil around newly planted roots is fine. When filling containers with soil a shake of the pot is enough; the potting mix will settle when it's thoroughly watered after planting.

If plants could talk I'm sure they'd agree with Aristotle: moderation in all things.

There are some who advise stomping on the soil when a plant is put in the ground. There's no need for fancy phrasing or footwork here: don't do it.

49. Whenever you put a plant in the ground, throw a handful of fertilizer into the bottom of the hole. And for bulbs, put bone meal in the bottom of the hole.

Imagine sitting down at a small table that, despite its reduced size, is filled with platters and bowls of delicious looking food. There are all types of edibles – vegetables, meats, fruit, grains, bread, cheeses and more. This table-for-one is heaped with everything a person could want to be satisfied and well nourished...if perhaps overfed. It's a *feast*, right?

> We're confining our plants to a tiny table filled with too much good food.

Now imagine that someone tells you that this is your food for a long time...maybe for years, and it *stays on that table*. If you leave, there is no food for you. Suddenly, what seemed like an incredible bounty isn't nearly enough and you can't live your life at that small tabletop, can you? It would be far better to have less over a longer period of time and be able to consume the food wherever you happen to be.

When throwing a concentrated amount of fertilizer into the bottom of a planting hole, we're confining our plants to a tiny table filled with too much food. Think about it: once the plant's roots begin to grow, they'll be out and far away from the concentrated fertilizer.

It's far better to scatter fertilizer over the entire bed where plants are to grow. If you're using an organic product it will release the nutrients slowly, over time, and assist your plants' growth continually as the root systems expand. When planting bulbs, scatter the organic bulb food over the whole area as well; when you dig the holes for each bulb, some of this fertilizer will get incorporated into the soil and the rest will amend the soil from the surface down.

If all the fertilizer is put in a concentrated pile at the bottom of a hole, it won't be near the roots as they grow into the soil. And if that fertilizer is a synthetic product it can burn the roots that are placed on top.

Wisdom from the Past

Sometimes it's true: the more things change the more they stay the same. This caution about adding fertilizer when planting appeared on the front page of the January 27, 1917 edition of the *El Paso herald*. Clearly, the author, G.A. Martin, was passionate about this topic, and though his link between manure and strychnine is a tad extreme, it does cause the reader to sit up and pay attention!

"Too much attention to plants when first put out is often the cause of many failures.

People kill more plants by putting manure or other fertilizer into the hole with the plant than in any other way.

No plant needs fertilizer the first few weeks or months after it is set out: the fertilizer merely burns it up.

Even the practice of putting manure down into the hole below the bottom of the hole in which the tree or plant is set, is dangerous, for it may be that this manure will not become thoroughly decomposed by the time the roots reach it and in that event, instead of affording sustenance to the plant or tree, it causes its death.

Manure is as dangerous to a plant as strychnine is to the human. Seldom will a plant die immediately for lack of food, but it will quickly die if given too much strong food."

Martin adds that often plants don't need to be fed before they are actively growing, during the middle of the season. *"Most trees and plants will go through the first season without any fertilizer, if any is needed, it will not be required until the middle of the summer at the earliest."*

G.A. Martin's advice is echoed in the Horticultural Hints column published in *The Pulaski citizen* in January of 1875. Here, the unknown author wrote, *"Do not, under any circumstances, add or apply any stimulating manure in the hole while planting."* The article continues, *"Where the ground is poor, an application of anything in the shape of manure on the surface around the tree is all that is necessary. On trees one or two years planted, add stimulating manure or withhold it, as the nature of the case calls for."*

50. Use Epsom salt on...(fill in the name of a plant).

When researching the use of Epsom salt in the garden I was reminded of an old Saturday Night Live sketch about "New Shimmer." "It's a floor wax!" the wife, played by Gilda Radner, insists. The husband, Dan Aykroyd, claims, "It's a dessert topping!" Naturally, the product was both.

Although I haven't seen Epsom salt recommended as either a floor wax or a dessert topping, it's been suggested for just about everything else. Through the years, advice columns, books, and now Internet sites have advocated using Epsom salt for tile cleaning, splinter removal, bath soaks, foot treatments, as a hair curling agent, laxative, facial hair remover, curtain stiffening, insecticide, fertilizer, headache cure, sunburn relief, treatment for insect bites, and for creating fake frost on windows.

More about that frost recipe later, but if the same product is recommended for curling hair and removing it, shouldn't that give a thinking person pause?

Epsom salt was named for a town in Surrey, England, where it was once produced by boiling down mineral-rich spring water. Although the crystalline structure looks rather like table salt, Epsom salt is actually magnesium sulfate and contains 10% magnesium and 6% sulfur.

> If your soils are lacking in any one element, use a balanced fertilizer.

When I'm asked if Epsom salt should be applied on lawns, around roses, in the vegetable garden, or on houseplants, my reply is always the same. "Is your soil deficient in magnesium?" Most people don't know; they've heard that they can put Epsom salt on plants but they don't understand what it is or why they might use it.

Let's get down and dirty about this. Connecting back to the fictional New Shimmer dessert topping for a moment, we might think of soil as we would a recipe for sweets. The ingredients for a tasty dessert need to be in the right proportions to make something delicious. Add too much cinnamon, baking soda or salt and the results would be inedible.

Soil also needs to be kept in balance. It's a complex community made of minerals, organic matter, fungi, bacteria, other microorganisms, air and water. Too much of any one of those elements can throw everything off so that plants don't grow as well. Most plants need the

There are some who would tell you to water houseplants with Epsom salt. But without knowing if your plants need excess magnesium, it's a risky thing to do. Instead of encouraging a flourishing plant you might throw everything out of balance. This beautiful Epiphyllum, for example, isn't triggered into flowering by Epsom salt or any other fertilizer; it's a period of long nights followed by increasing hours of daylight that bring it into bloom every April.

magnesium and sulfur that's in Epsom salt, but unless you've tested the dirt you don't know if your soil already has these elements or not.

So why not just give a plant Epsom salts and see what happens? In response, I think of two popular sayings. The first is Barry Commoner's second law of ecology: "Everything must go somewhere." It's important to remember that products we put in our yards and gardens don't just vanish. When we put anything into our environment it ultimately ends up *somewhere*, and that's often downstream. So, better not to use something in the garden unless we know it's really needed.

The second phrase that comes to mind is, "If it ain't broke don't fix it." If the plants are growing well, chances are they are happy with the current conditions. Should you see that your plants aren't doing well, identify the problem first, and then consider all possible solutions. If you suspect the difficulty starts at ground level, have a compete soil test done before taking action.

When you're unsure if your soils are lacking in any one element, use a complete, organic fertilizer. A balanced fertilizer with all the essentials that plants require is less likely to throw Mother Nature's recipe off kilter.

Epsom salt is great for fashioning instant frost on windows, even when the weather is warm. Create instant privacy, write an easily washable message, or decorate for the holidays…just don't routinely add Epsom salt to plants.

In *The Closing Circle*, published in 1971, Barry Commoner wrote these four laws of ecology that are worth remembering today. In and out of the garden, these are wise words.

Everything Is Connected to Everything Else.
Everything Must Go Somewhere.
Nature Knows Best.
There Is No Such Thing as a Free Lunch.

Epsom Salts Window Frost

Because of Epsom salt's crystalline nature, it will form frost-like patterns on windows or mirrors when dissolved in liquid and painted on glass. This can be fun for holiday decorating or creating winter scenes.

You'll see many recipes for Epsom salt frost calling for beer as the liquid, but there seems to be no reason for this; perhaps someone was looking for a way to use up flat beer. The recipe works well with water so your house doesn't have to smell like a brewery.

½ cup water
½ cup Epsom salt
3 or 4 drops dishwashing detergent
(this helps the "frost" stick on the glass)

Bring the water to a boil in a saucepan. Remove from the heat and add the Epsom salt, stirring until it is completely dissolved. Add the drops of detergent and stir again. Let this mixture cool down before using or it will drip excessively, but apply before it starts to crystalize in the pan. Paint or daub it on your glass surface using a paintbrush, cotton ball, micro-fiber cloth, or even your finger.

Insects, Diseases
&
Other Problems

—⁓—

*"My green thumb came only as
a result of the mistakes I made while
learning to see things from
the plant's point of view.."*

– H. Fred Ale

51. I need to do something before this spreads.

There are some things that are highly contagious: yawning, applause, cold viruses, gossip, smiling and the measles, to name just a few. Home landscapers are often concerned that insect or disease damage is just as transmittable. They worry that a problem might spread from plant to plant as quickly as a cold sweeps through an elementary school.

We tend to think of plant problems as being similar to human illness, so it's understandable that people want to stop a difficulty before it affects the entire landscape. Reasonable as that seems, there are several arguments for pausing before taking action.

> There are several arguments for pausing before taking action.

First of all, this myth encourages us to proceed before getting a diagnosis. Is the problem you see caused by insects, disease, or a cultural situation such as being too wet or too dry? Until an accurate identification has been made, treatment might be a waste of time and money.

Many disease and insect problems in plants are host-specific. A group of plants might be prone to a particular disease while other plants remain resistant. The summer phlox in my perennial bed might get powdery mildew, for example, but the rest of the garden isn't bothered by this fungus.

Insects often feast on a certain plant or family of plants and leave all others alone. I can pretty much guarantee that in late summer my butterfly weed will be covered with orange aphids. These are called *Asclepias* aphids because they attack members of this plant genus. I only see this insect on members of the milkweed family, however, so I know that I won't find the rest of my garden covered in orange bugs.

If the situation is caused by cultural conditions – what's been happening around a plant – no amount of fungicide or insecticide will help. Plants wilting of drought, or those that are suffering from herbicide damage, won't be helped by a pesticide. So applying even a fairly benign product without knowing a problem's cause might be the equivalent of pouring that product down the drain. Not only is it wasteful, it can also be detrimental to your garden. Pesticides kill indiscriminately; beneficial insects and fungi are usually killed along with the target pests. Knocking out the good guys along with the bad can throw nature's balance out of whack, resulting in a landscape that's ripe for other pests and problems.

Every year I see these orange aphids on my butterfly weed, but I don't worry that they will spread to all the plants in my gardens. This aphid prefers to target plants in the Asclepias family. I ignore these aphids, leaving them for other critters to eat.

We often notice damage in our yards and gardens long after the cause has come and gone. Many diseases and insects have specific periods when they're active or precise conditions they need to thrive. We see fungus on evergreen foliage in the spring that actually spotted the leaves the previous summer. We notice chewed plants that were damaged by night-feeding insects several weeks ago; that population of pests might be long gone. There is no point in treating problems well after they've occurred and are no longer of concern.

Finally, it's important to remember that in the landscape there is always an acceptable level of damage. No one's yard and garden is without injury and difficulty and in many instances we don't have to act. I don't bother to treat that

Lace bug is an insect that feeds on plant juices. There are species of lace bug that attack andromeda (Pieris japonica), such as this plant, and those that cause similar stippling on rhododendrons, elm and sycamore, to name just a few. Although these insects can discolor foliage and reduce plant vigor, it's reassuring that they'll be controlled with horticultural oil and they won't spread to every other plant on the property.

mildew on the summer phlox or the orange aphids on my *Asclepias* plants.

We might appreciate a cure for the common cold, but as long as we've planted landscapes containing a diverse population of plants we don't have to worry that a problem will sweep through the yard and garden.

Wisdom From The Past

In *How to Make The Garden Pay*, written by T. Greiner and published by Wm. Henry Maule in 1894, the author gives this advice that is still sound today.

"PREVENTATIVE TREATMENTS – First of all, the prudent gardener will take precautionary measures against infection. Strict rotation stands foremost. He will remove his endangered crops to new fields, and as far remote as possible from infected ground."

Greiner counsels that any plant that's had a problem should be removed from the garden.

"Keeping the premises free from weeds, and rubbish, and burning wastes and refuse, such as potato tops, old tomato vines, dead weeds, leaves, etc., with all the spores that have found a lodging place on these materials, will close another avenue by which infection so frequently is given a chance to enter.

"Another important precautionary measure is the selection of resistant varieties, if any such are known and the fortification of all plants against the attacks of diseases by good culture and judicious feeding. Strong growing plants are less subject to some diseases than are plants with weakened vitality."

Household cleaners make good garden remedies.

One of the most memorable characters in *My Big Fat Greek Wedding* is the father of the bride who uses Windex as a cure for everything. Cuts, acne, sprains...every physical ailment got a spray of the blue window cleaner. Movie viewers found this amusing, but it's not an approach we want to copy, on our bodies or in the garden. Unfortunately, when some people see a problem in their landscape, they too reach under the kitchen sink.

> When something is amiss in the landscape, get an accurate diagnosis first.

Sometimes the impulse to use a cleaning product is based in fact but ignores the complexities involved. For example, common household ammonia is rich in nitrogen. Yet this doesn't mean it makes a good fertilizer, since ammonia is also quite volatile and the nitrogen isn't easily available to plants. Ammonia can turn soil very alkaline as well, making other nutrients unattainable.

Similarly, knowing that insecticidal soap is commonly used to treat insect infestations, some might reach for the bottle of dish detergent. Products made for washing dishes have other ingredients, however, and these may not be good for plants. Detergents are not the same as pure soap. We need to remember that components that are fine in a household cleaner might dry foliage or make leaves more sensitive to sunburn.

This is an easy myth to think about logically. If something goes wrong with your car you wouldn't pour bleach, ammonia or detergent in the gas tank and hope that it will solve the problem. That would be a waste of the cleaner and might do more harm than good, right?

Your garden is a complicated, finely tuned engine too, although it doesn't run on gasoline. When something is amiss in the landscape, get an accurate diagnosis first. If treatment is necessary, find an appropriate product intended for plants and use it according to the directions.

Is any product that comes in a white bottle as powerful and effective outdoors as it is on a dirty house? Probably not, and household products can actually be harmful to plants.

Put chewing gum in the hole of a woodchuck... he'll eat it, it clogs his intestines and he'll die.

The origins of this myth are obscure, but I imagine that gum manufacturers were very pleased when it first appeared in garden almanacs and newspapers. Unfortunately, there is more wishful thinking here than wisdom.

Woodchucks, aka groundhogs, have plagued gardeners since vegetable gardens were first cultivated in North America. I found a comment about this animal in an 1875 issue of the *Washington D.C. Evening Star* that says it all. "The moral delinquency of the ground hog can never be sufficiently condemned," the unidentified columnist wrote.

Although I probably wouldn't call this animal morally delinquent, I'm sympathetic with this statement. Years ago, I went into our vegetable garden and noticed broccoli plant damage. They weren't just nibbled, which is what rabbits do, and the tops weren't grazed, which is typical of deer damage. These plants were gone, eaten down to the nubs. We had a woodchuck.

> Keep the Tabasco in the kitchen and the gum in your mouth.

"I'll fix that critter," I thought, and went into my kitchen for a jar of Tabasco. I sprinkled hot sauce all over the remaining plants, enjoying the thought of a groundhog with its mouth on fire. The next day those Tabasco coated plants were also missing. It was clear that the woodchuck had just thought it was Mexican Night.

Groundhogs that find gum might think they've moved to Candy Land, but it won't either kill them or cause them to move on. And no, the brand of gum isn't what's important. Exterminators have often reported that when they visit a property to trap and remove a woodchuck, they find all types of gum, wrapped and unwrapped, lying around the animal's den.

Keep the Tabasco in the kitchen and the gum in your mouth. Fencing, traps, repellants and motion-activated sprinklers are more effective than chewing gum.

How much gum could a woodchuck chew if a woodchuck could chew gum? Large or small amounts, wrapped or unwrapped, bubble or Juicy Fruit®...it really doesn't matter because groundhogs don't chew gum.

There is an easy way to control weeds, if you just use *this* product.

This is a true story about a new gardener whose first perennial garden was a bit too ambitious. She'd moved into a newly built house where a large slope next to the driveway was slightly too steep for a lawn. "We'll make it into a perennial garden," she said, envisioning this thirty-by-fifty-foot field filled with colorful flowers.

> There isn't a single silver bullet.

Not only was this a big space to plant, but also the soil was filled with decades' worth of weed seeds. At the time, this gardener didn't know that seeds could remain viable but dormant for many, many years. The old saying, "One year seeding makes nine years weeding," is actually optimistic.

How long can weed seeds live? Let's just say that your garden contains weed seeds from the *Nixon* administration that are able to sprout. They are tiny, ticking time bombs awaiting the perfect combination of light, temperature and water that will trigger their germination.

As this young gardener was happily turning the soil to plant perennials, sleeping seeds were being activated. In the coming years she had the opportunity to learn a great deal about weed control.

First, she discovered that mulch will shade many weed seeds, preventing their germination. A layer of two or three inches of bark mulch was pretty effective in that garden, but the annual application was time-consuming work. And after the expense and effort of spreading mulch, she was dismayed to find that there were still weeds to pull.

Here is one of the problems with landscape fabric. Weeds germinate in the mulch on top of the fabric and their roots grow through the porous barrier down into the soil. Similarly, the roots of shrubs and trees go up into the fabric to reach the decomposing mulch on top. Consequently, when weeds are pulled the fabric rips, and when the fabric is removed it damages roots of desirable plantings.

Secondly, she found that although there are products for preventing seed germination – called pre-emergent herbicides – they must be used exactly as directed on the label. The timing and amount applied is important. Some of these products are toxic to aquatic life and they can damage some perennial plants. She also discovered that pre-emergent products don't kill existing weeds. All in all, this gardener decided that pre-emergents weren't for her.

Next, she learned that herbicides that killed weeds on contact also destroy other plants they touch. It's nearly impossible to spray herbicides on weeds without harming neighboring perennials and shrubs. And she had concerns about where the ingredients in such weed killers end up and how safe they are for people, pets, and the environment. Contact herbicides weren't of interest for this flowerbed, she determined.

So our gardener tried landscape fabric. This worked initially, but later became a garden nightmare. The fabric prevented the mulch that covered it from decomposing into the soil. This halted one of the benefits mulching, which is amending the garden from the top down. Weed seeds that blew into the garden were happy to germinate in the decomposing mulch that was on top of the fabric. When she pulled these weeds out, their roots – which permeated the barrier – tore the fabric.

After being left with a garden of torn, unsightly and inefficient old fabric, she began the arduous task of pulling it out of the garden. At that point, this ever-more-experienced gardener found that the roots of perennials, shrubs and trees had grown up *into* the cloth as well, and the fabric removal had damaged the roots of nearby plants.

Our gardener ultimately discovered what long-time gardeners know: although there are several products and practices that can help with weed control, nothing is perfect and many have their cautions or disadvantages. There isn't a single silver bullet.

Perhaps your experience with weeds has been similar. I was that young gardener. After many years of trial and error, I settled on the combination of bark mulch, vigilance, and hand pulling as my method of weed control. At least three times a year I spent a full day pulling weeds that broke through the mulch, and in those weeding sessions I came to believe that weeds are actually a gift.

Had it not been for those weeds, I wouldn't have spent five minutes sitting in that garden, let alone several hours. Nothing else takes us into our gardens in the same way as getting eye-to-eye with our plants, in direct contact with the earth.

Did You Know...

Crabgrass Grows Anywhere

Which is why it was originally brought to this country as a grain crop. Crabgrass is a form of millet that's native to central Europe. Immigrants from Eastern Europe brought it with them because it was reliable and adaptable. Once those farmers got access to grains that were easier to grow and harvest, such as wheat and corn, they discarded the millet. Their dependable millet grew on, becoming our consistent weed.

Corn Gluten For Weed Control

Although corn gluten was once lauded as an organic pre-emergent herbicide, using it for this purpose is tricky for most gardeners. Corn gluten does prevent a weed from growing roots when it germinates, but only if the newly sprouted seed is then kept dry. If it rains in the days after germination, or an irrigation system comes on, the weed sprouts will go on to root and grow.

Corn gluten needs to be applied before weed seeds germinate and then watered in well. If weeds have already sprouted, the corn gluten will just fertilize these young plants. So in order for this organic pre-emergent to work, the gardener must be sure that they're putting the corn down before most weed seeds sprout and in a period when rain isn't expected. This need for precise timing makes corn gluten too complicated for most people to rely on.

Directed Watering

Beds where it's practical to use drip irrigation will have fewer weeds. Overhead irrigation of vegetable gardens and flower beds dampens open soil, helping weed seeds to germinate and grow. If the spaces in between your vegetables or perennials aren't watered there will be fewer weeds in those areas.

10-Minute Weeding

No, all of your weed problems won't be solved in ten minutes. But you can pull a surprising amount of weeds in that amount of time. People are often overwhelmed by weeding because they're approaching it as an all-or-nothing task. If they don't have an entire day to spend clearing a bed, they don't even begin.

Pulling weeds in short bursts of time can be a better approach. Ten minutes here or a half an hour there mounts up, ultimately resulting in weed control. Use weed pulling as a decompression period after work or while making phone calls. Pull a few weeds as you walk past a garden or pick vegetables for dinner.

55. Watering plants when it's sunny causes burn spots on the leaves.

It's common knowledge that a lens can be used to direct a beam of light so concentrated it can start a fire. Magnifying glasses are used for such purposes in school science classes, instructions given in outdoor camping manuals, and pocket-size lenses sold in wilderness survival stores. Girl and Boy Scouts the world over can tell you how to burn a hole in paper using ice, a pair of glasses, or a shard of clear glass.

So it's no wonder that people move this widespread wisdom into the garden. Seeing clear drops of water on leaves after a rain, and noticing brown spots on foliage that look like burn marks, they make the leap from A to B and deduce C. The sun must be burning the holes through the magnifying drops of water, right? Therefore, watering on a sunny day will make scald dots on your leaves.

It all sounds logical enough, but that's not what happens. As any child who has done the experiment in science class can tell you, that concentrated beam of light isn't produced if you put the magnifying glass right on top of the paper. The lens has to be held at the right distance and angle to produce a beam focused enough to burn.

We also know that the brown spots on foliage are made by fungi. Water does play a role here, however; many a fungus that produces spotted leaves thrives in moisture. Several studies show that frequent splashing of water onto foliage promotes the growth of fungi that cause these spots. Sunlight, however, has nothing to do with it.

> Brown spots on foliage are usually made by fungi.

In fact, plants that get splashed in the very early morning when it's cool, or in the evening when they're less likely to dry quickly, are more prone to the problem. In general, it's best to water plants in the morning; the hours before sunrise aren't necessarily ideal because moisture is more apt to linger.

Irrigation systems that are set to come on frequently are practically a prescription for leaf spot. In some gardens you can tell where sprinklers are located by noticing which sides of the hosta or hydrangeas are filled with leaf spot. While it's not always practical to water with soaker hoses and keep foliage dry, it is possible to set sprinklers to come on for longer periods of time less frequently. This is especially important for plants whose leaves don't shed water quickly.

The good news is that usually leaf spots are a cosmetic problem. Few plants die from spotted foliage, although once enough of the leaf is contaminated and it's not as useful for photosynthesis, the plant may discard that foliage.

Certainly watering during the heat of the day isn't conducive to the efficient use of water, as some of it evaporates into the air. If plants are thirsty when the sun is out, however, by all means water them.

Wisdom From the Past

With one major exception, the advice on watering found in *Yard and Garden*, by Tarkington Parker, is as applicable to home landscapers today as it was in 1908 when the book was published.

The author recommends planning a garden so that plants with similar needs for water are placed in the same location. "Group those flowers demanding much moisture together as nearly as possible and those demanding less moisture in groups distinct from the others."

In addition to this sound instruction Parker says, "Moreover, when water is applied, let the application be thorough. It does very little good to sprinkle the beds with a light mist from the hose or watering can; this may often freshen the foliage after a hot, burning day, but it gives no water to the roots, where the moisture is necessary."

The one part of Parker's advice that can be ignored is his insistence that gardens should be watered at night. He goes so far as to say that "to water the beds in the late morning or early afternoon is dangerous, if not altogether fatal." Fatal! The author didn't explain why a rainfall at the same time of day isn't killing off plants.

It isn't ideal to water in the middle of a sunny day, since more of the water will evaporate instead of soaking into the soil. But watering when it's sunny won't cause burn spots on plants – and if your garden is wilting in hot, dry conditions, it's not going to hurt to turn the sprinkler on.

56. Moss in your lawn means you need to lime.

If you walk into most garden centers in America and tell them that you have moss in the lawn, what are they going to sell you? That's right…a bag of lime. The myth is this: if you have moss in your lawn, it means your soil is acidic. The truth is that moss will happily grow right on limestone rocks, so why would an application of lime deter it from flourishing on turf?

Andrew Weidman, a garden writer and naturalist, talks about the pH of soil in his region. "South Central Pennsylvania is known for its massive bluestone lime deposits, which originally attracted German immigrants to settle here. They knew that bluestone meant that the soil would be very fertile."

"Abandoned Colonial and early Federal lime kilns dot the countryside in this area," Andrew continues, "and lime quarries for crushed stone and quicklime make up a major part of the local economy. This underlying stone has rendered our soils so sweet that blueberries cannot easily grow here. And yet mosses grow quite happily in our forests and along our streams, apparently unaware that they cannot survive such alkaline conditions!"

> Moss is happy to grow on either acid or alkaline soils.

Moss thrives in shade and moist locations. It can grow well on compact or infertile soil and is often found on stones, rotting logs, and the base of tree trunks on their shady side. Remember those mysteries and adventure stories where the protagonist finds his or her way out of the woods by looking for moss on the north (shady) side of the trees?

You may or may not need to lime your lawn in order for your grass to thrive. Only a soil test will show if the pH is in the 6 to 7 range that's ideal for turf growth. If you have moss, however, it's likely that the soil is compact, the area is shady, or the surface of the ground is moist. Any or all of these circumstances favors moss.

To address the conditions that produce mosses, aerate the area and top-dress with compost to address the compaction, thin out surrounding vegetation to lessen the shade, and be sure that you aren't watering the lawn any more often than every four days. Alternatively, you can leave things as they are and accept the moss as the best plant for the area. Why fight to grow grass in shade when mosses are the better plant for the job?

Even after spreading lime every year, a homeowner may be distressed to find moss growing. Moss flourishes here because the soil is compact and the area is shady. In order to get rid of the moss, those conditions need to be changed...or the lawn's owner can accept that perhaps in this shady yard the moss is the better green carpet.

57. A compacted lawn can be aerated with spiked shoes.

You have to admire human ingenuity. We're constantly inventing new items and improving on established ones. People have submitted patent applications for all types of shoe enhancements, for example. There are shoes with tiny umbrellas that keep the toes dry, shoes with springs in the heels, and footgear with built-in shoehorns. Patents have been filed for shoes with built-in ladder gripping devices and small air conditioning units in the heels.

Someone has invented slippers with handles sticking out the heels so that the shoe becomes a cockroach swatter. Another has created footwear with a small broom on one shoe and a tiny dustpan on the toe of the other. There are slippers that have dust mops on their soles, made for humans and for cats as well. (Show me a cat that will go along with that one!)

Finally, and my personal favorite for The Museum of the Hard to Believe, are the shoes with hollow heels that connect with a catheter for holding the wearer's urine. Don't ask.

> Save the fancy footwear for other occasions.

When I was taking a photo of these spiked sandals on the lawn, Riley couldn't stay away from them. "They're on the grass and they're plastic," he seems to be thinking, "so maybe they're a dog toy?"

All of these make the variety of spiked shoe designs look downright sensible. There are cleated shoes for improving performance in a number of sports. Patents have also been filed for various types of spiked shoes to wear on ice and other hazardous terrains. So why not make those spikes just a bit longer so that your turf is aerated as you walk on the grass or mow the lawn?

Let's ignore the difficulty in walking with two to three-inch spikes coming out of the soles, as well as the danger of stabbing your other foot. The main problem here is that as a spike enters the ground it creates a hole by compressing the soil on all sides of that barb. So although a small hole is created, it is done by compacting the soil more. The people who designed aeration equipment long ago recognized that the best way to lighten compacted soil is by removing a plug right out of the ground, not packing the dirt into itself.

Some may argue that these spiked sandals are good for killing grubs when worn during the months when they are close to the surface of turf. I suppose this is possible, although the odds of hitting substantial numbers of grubs are probably pretty low, and there is an equal potential for harming earthworms and beneficial insects.

For a healthy lawn, aerate with a machine that removes plugs of soil, allow grass clippings to fall back onto the turf when you mow, and save the fancy footwear for other occasions.

Did You Know...

- Homeowners can reduce the compaction of soil by not mowing or walking on the lawn when the ground is wet, and by periodically altering mowing patterns.

- We tend to think of a lawn as an area and forget that it's actually made up of individual, and extremely tolerant, plants. What other plant would we expect to thrive even as we cut it down close to the ground on a weekly basis? Like all plants, the leaves are the food factories that make energy for the grass plants. The larger these leaves are, the more energy they produce. So in order to keep turf flourishing, you'll want to mow high. Cut your lawn between 2 ½ to 3 inches tall so your grass will be as healthy as possible.

- Too much water can be as stressful to lawns as not enough. It is usually a contributing factor in various lawn diseases. Also, frequent, shallow watering is a prescription for moss growth and grubs. Moist conditions nurture mosses and beetles love to lay their eggs, which transform into root-eating grubs, in damp soil. Water your lawn deeply once a week or even less frequently, but for a longer period of time. If you have an automatic irrigation system, be sure that it has the ability to measure rain and shut off if nature has already watered.

58. Goldenrod causes hay fever.

Remember the kid in middle school who got blamed for any disturbance, whether he was at fault or not? Chances are he stood out in some way; he was louder, more active, taller, or impulsive. When the teacher's back was turned and the class burst into laughter, that kid's name was the first out of the instructor's lips.

> Ragweed is the kid who actually throws the pollen-spitballs.

Kudos to those garden centers who sell Solidago. Many shy away from this sturdy, late-blooming perennial because they mistakenly think that the yellow flower causes hay fever.

Goldenrod *(Solidago)* must feel like that child. This showy flower gets blamed for causing hay fever and every other late-summer allergy. It is banned from bouquets, pulled from flower-beds, and sprayed with roadside herbicides. Yes, this lovely, robust perennial is the wild child who stands out in the summer landscape and is therefore unfairly accused of causing sinus problems.

There are over one hundred species in the genus *Solidago* and more than seventy are native to North America. In late summer and early fall, yellow goldenrod flowers joyously bloom in ditches, fields, and occasionally in flower gardens.

Solidago has been used medicinally and as a dye plant by Native Americans and immigrants alike. Poets have sung its praises, it's been harvested and shipped to China for tea, and used to make perfumes and jelly. Goldenrod is the state flower of Kentucky and Nebraska.

Even as the majority of people see it only as a common weed, commercial growers for the floral industry raise it for the cut flower market. Although goldenrod is largely ignored or disdained in the United States, it is a valued perennial for flower gardens in Europe and the British Isles. *Solidago* is a great plant for butterfly and cutting gardens; there are varieties for every landscape, ranging from six inches to over six feet tall.

To its detriment, this easy to grow perennial stands out in a crowd. It is conspicuously in flower at the same time as the less showy ragweed *(Ambrosia)* whose small, greenish flowers are nearly invisible in the landscape. So while the lightweight, imperceptible ragweed pollen blows into nostrils, causing allergic rhinitis, the conspicuous goldenrod pollen gets blamed. The *Solidago's* pollen is not only more noticeable, it's also too large and waxy to become airborne. In fact, goldenrod needs to be insect pollinated because it doesn't blow in the wind.

Ragweed is the kid who actually throws the pollen-spitballs, but keeps his eyes on his desk and book while the teacher blames the usual scapegoat. Goldenrod is ragweed's fall guy.

Desirable Varieties of Goldenrod

There are many lovely species and types of *Solidago*, but these four are particularly good performers, gathering raves from gardeners and high ratings

from the Chicago Botanic Garden. You can find the complete report about all the *Solidago* varieties tested at the CBG on their website, www.chicagobotanic.org. Ask your local garden center about which *Solidago* varieties they carry, but many are also available for order online. Most goldenrods are hardy in USDA planting zones 4-9.

Image courtesy of the Oklahoma Historical Society.

S. 'Baby Sun'

This is one of the earliest goldenrod varieties to bloom. It's usually in flower from early July until mid August and grows to just over 2' tall and 3' wide.

S. 'Goldkind' (aka Golden Baby)

Growing to just two feet tall, 'Goldkind' was developed for the cut flower business in Europe. This variety flowers from late July through September and is a sturdy plant that doesn't need staking. 'Goldkind' has thick, showy flower plumes and is great for the front to mid section of the perennial border.

S. rugosa 'Fireworks'

Probably the most widely available goldenrod, 'Fireworks' grows to about 4' tall and 6' wide. Give this plant room to strut its stuff! The flowers on 'Fireworks' are thinner and more delicate than many goldenrods are, making it more desirable for those who don't want a perennial that screams "Hello, *yellow!*" and dominates the garden. 'Fireworks' is also a popular variety for cutting gardens. This type of *Solidago* is in flower from mid September to late October.

S. Sphacelata 'Golden Fleece'

One of the shorter growing goldenrods, 'Golden Fleece' works well in a perennial garden, as a groundcover or in a wildflower meadow. It grows 18" to 2' tall and about 3' wide. 'Golden Fleece' is in flower for about two months, starting in late August.

Goldenrod makes a perfect companion to other late-season perennials in the flower garden. It's also perfect for bouquets, so be sure to plant enough to harvest as a cut flower.

Random Folklore

—⁓—

"It is only when you start a garden – probably after age fifty – that you realize something important happens every day."

– Geoffrey B. Charlesworth

59. Lawns and gardens do best with daily watering.

Are you raising spoiled brats? Are you indulging those in your care to the point where they can't take care of themselves? Have you thought that showering them with whatever they want is a good thing, only to see that you've produced overindulged horrors?

> Frequent watering of plants creates an assortment of problems.

No, you haven't stumbled into a chapter on child rearing...we're still talking about plants. The consequences of overindulgence are similar, however. Frequent watering of plants creates an assortment of problems.

This photo shows just one problem with automatic irrigation systems that come on daily: on this windy day more water was being blown away than was reaching the ground. A deep soaking less often promotes deep root systems and allows the surface of the soil to dry.

George Glenny's paragraph in the sidebar, written in 1880, spells it out perfectly. Frequent watering only dampens the surface of the soil and this leads to shallow root systems. If your lawn or garden is watered daily for a short time, plants will develop roots on the surface of the soil that dry out quickly.

When his book was written, daily watering was accomplished with a garden hose or cans. Frequent hand watering remains problematic today because people get bored long before their plants are soaked deeply. In the 21st century, poor programming of automatic irrigation is also at fault. Many people have set their systems to water for a short period every day. This only moistens the top couple of inches of soil.

In addition to shallow roots, frequent irrigation is a prescription for every fungal problem in the book. From brown patch and red thread on turf to leaf spot on shrubs and perennials, too much water creates the perfect environment for diseases. Although not a disease, daily irrigation also promotes the growth of moss in lawns and flowerbeds, even in sunny areas.

Gardeners knew about "tough love" in 1880 and it remains true today: infrequent, deep soakings are better than a brief daily soaking.

From *A Year's Work in Garden and Greenhouse*, by George Glenny, published in 1880.

"Watering. This is an operation that requires repeating frequently during the month, but it ought only to be resorted to in the greatest emergency. Unless things are perceptibly suffering for want of it, it ought not to be made a practice of; it is the commencement of bad habits. Plants, like people, may be spoiled: help them, and they will not help themselves; teach them self-reliance, and they make shift without assistance. As an example, if we begin watering plants the roots no longer go down after moisture—they come up after it, and we are forced to continue it; but if we are obliged to water, let the whole space of the ground be watered alike, the same as a heavy shower of rain would do it. Common surface watering is worse than none. The farce of sprinkling the ground that it may look black and wet for an hour is amusing enough to those who know better, but, as we have always said, a thorough good watering once a week is far better than the ordinary sprinkling of the surface once a day."

60. Daffodils poison tulips in the vase.

This myth comes with a confession about the accompanying photograph. While it is true that tulips will wilt when placed in a vase with daffodils, I was in a hurry and couldn't wait for these to droop. Full disclosure: I took the daffodils out of the pitcher and shoved the tulips in the microwave.

Had I been more patient, the tulips would have withered on their own, but not because the daffodils were secreting something toxic. Bacteria, not nasty *Narcissus*, are the culprits here.

If you've ever cut daffodils from your yard you've probably noticed how the stems drip sap as you walk back to the house. Members of the genus *Narcissus* are juicy plants. That liquid is full of sugar, and what loves to grow in sugary plant sap? Bacteria. Tulips are just a bit more sensitive to these stem-clogging bacteria than the daffodils are, so they will usually wilt first.

Gardeners and flower arrangers should feel free to make arrangements from all the spring flowers they wish. Go ahead and create the lovely lift-our-hearts bouquets you crave at this time of year. Just remember to use a floral

> Tulips are more sensitive to stem-clogging bacteria.

preservative in the vase, or change the water every day, to keep bacteria at bay.

Some people hesitate to put these two spring flowers together because they've heard that daffodils will poison the tulips. It's not that Narcissus are nasty...they're just less prone to wilting when bacteria breeds in the water and clogs the stems.

61. In winter, mist houseplants or set the pots on trays of rocks to increase humidity around plants.

This myth probably generates more plant guilt than any other. "I should be misting these houseplants," people think every winter. We've read that houseplants need a high level of humidity in order to thrive. We buy plant misters but never get around to using them. We feel bad that we're not giving our plants an ideal environment.

> Misting doesn't appreciably raise the humidity around plants.

You may have heard that instead of misting you can place a tray of pebbles under the pots and fill it with water. I have installed several of these and immediately felt virtuous. Then the dead leaves from the plants dropped into the trays and began rotting in the water. This plant debris mixed with household dust and soon I was brewing a dank, primordial soup. Guilt surfaced again; I was surrounding my plants with alternate life forms instead of moisture!

It will be a relief to everyone to learn that sporadic misting and trays of water don't appreciably raise the humidity around plants. The only way to substantially increase a room's level of moisture is with a humidifier.

The bottom line is that most houseplants cope pretty well with dry winter air. Don't focus on humidity…drop the level of guilt.

Yes, in winter there is less humidity in the house but the plants themselves are the answer. A good selection of houseplants will help raise the level of moisture in the air, and you don't have to worry about misting or placing the plants on trays of pebbles and water.

62. You have to break up or cut a root ball before you put a plant in the ground.

There are many people who assume that all sushi is made of raw fish. In fact, the word sushi refers to the vinegared rice and means something like "sour rice." Over time, however, many people have come to believe that because some or all these delicious rolls are made with raw fish, all sushi contains uncooked seafood.

Moving from Japanese cuisine to ancient Rome, it's also widely assumed that houses at that period were built with a vomitorium where those who had overindulged during a feast could purge before eating more. In actuality, a vomitorium was the entranceway where the large crowds passed on their way into and out of a stadium. The word comes from a Latin verb meaning "to spew forth." In architecture, the word refers to allowing many people to enter and exit quickly.

Some myths or misunderstandings start with a truth that then gets applied in a wider, inappropriate manner. In gardening, breaking or cutting a root ball is one of these. There are a couple of instances when it is good to cut roots before planting, but not all root balls need such disruption.

The most important root pruning is done to trees and large shrubs that have been growing in a container for too long. In these cases, the roots can circle around the pot to such an extent that later, as the trunk grows, those encircling roots actually strangle the plant.

> Not all root balls need such disruption.

I was on a garden consultation once where the homeowners asked me to look at a *Gingko* tree that had been growing in their yard for several years. It was about 6' tall and it was dead. The wife and daughter were blaming something the husband had done in the area for this tree's demise. He didn't think he was responsible, but felt bad because this was a sentimental plant for the entire family.

"We had these on the tables at my daughter's wedding," his wife explained. "After the reception, people took them home and planted them, but I think only a few of the trees are still alive."

I bent down and pulled the soil away from the bottom of the trunk, looking to see if a mouse or vole had eaten the bark near the base. Instead of tooth marks, however, I saw a girdling root.

"Were these trees in bonsai dishes?" I asked, and was told that they were indeed bonsai

Gingko trees. "It was the small dish that killed this tree," I told this couple. "When it was in that tiny container one of the main roots wrapped around the stem and strangled the plant all these years later."

Shrubs and trees should be inspected for circling or girdling roots, and these should be cut before the plant is put in the ground. If the roots aren't seen to be growing around and around in the pot, they don't need to be loosened.

Some small annuals might develop equally congested root balls, especially if they've been growing in six-packs for an extended period. If the mass of roots is so thick that you have a hard time seeing brown dirt, pull some of the roots out from the bottom in order to loosen them.

The majority of plants aren't so rootbound that you need to pull, cut or otherwise disturb the roots. In fact, plants are pretty smart when it comes to root growth. Roots will stop and shift directions when coming to a barrier, for example. In most cases we don't need to pull them apart.

We humans are good at taking what we know and then assuming that we know everything. From sushi, vomitoriums, and cutting up roots, we see that sometimes our assumptions are overextended to the point where they've grown beyond the truth.

Not all roots need to be loosened when a plant is put in the ground. A good rule of thumb is how many white roots you see and whether they ring the inside of the pot. If there are more roots than dirt visible, or if they circle around and around, pull them apart so they won't stay congested after planting.

63. Always put a layer of rocks or clay shards in the bottom of a pot "for drainage."

Change isn't easy and habits are challenging to break. Sometimes we resist a new practice simply because admitting that we were wrong, or were doing something needlessly, is difficult.

When it comes to this myth, however, change we must. For years we've been told a layer of rocks or broken clay pottery into the bottom of a pot "for drainage." Many people also place a larger rock or piece of screening over the bottom hole so that the dirt or pebbles won't leak out.

It's time we all acknowledge that putting anything but soil at the bottom of the pot is a nuisance, unnecessary, and *bad for plants*.

Rocks and shards are annoying because when you move the plant to a larger container, or empty out the pot into the garden or compost, those rocks and shards usually need to be removed. They are unnecessary, because when it comes to drainage, *that's what the hole in the bottom of the pot is for*.

Anyone who has seen what roots do inside a pot knows why rocks and shards are bad for plants. Roots grow down into containers, circling

> Putting anything at the bottom of the pot is bad for plants.

around the bottom and perimeter of the pot. They don't stop when they reach the so-called drainage layers, but end up in rocks and shards instead of in the soil where roots belong.

Covering drainage holes defeats their purpose and is pointless because very little potting mix or dirt escapes from these openings.

Potting soil alone should fill a container top to bottom and those who find this tough to accept should head to the nearest garden center. See all of those potted plants in the nurseries and greenhouses? There isn't a rock or shard in the bottom of *any* of those containers. If a "drainage layer" or the covering of holes were necessary, don't you think the professional growers would be doing it?

This photo shows why rocks or shards in the bottom of a pot are bad for plants. Roots grow down into that "drainage layer" where there is no soil, no water and no nutrients.

When a plant is grown in a pot, roots will circle around and grow all the way to the bottom of the container. They don't stop when they reach the bottom. In fact, once roots start to grow out of the drainage hole as they were in this container, it's time to repot, without rocks or shards in the bottom!

64. Frost is more likely when there is a full moon.

When someone asks me to name a few of the topics in my book, my usual answer has been, "Oh, things like frost is more likely on a full moon." There's always a pause before the questioner says, "You mean that isn't *true*?" A look at data, and thinking

> Common sense tells us that this folklore is fiction.

about the variety of topography in any single area, shows why this myth is made of moonbeams.

In the spring and fall, a frost is more likely to occur on clear nights. But several people have collected data of first and last frosts in their area and then compared it to the phases of the moon. They found no correlation between a full moon and frost. Even without this assessment of the numbers, common sense tells us that this folklore is fiction.

A quick online search of average first and last frost dates shows tremendous variation from one area to another. In Presque Isle, Maine, for example, the

A newly frosted garden has a certain beauty, even if we're sad to see plants die. But the degree of cold and the timing of hard frosts have nothing to do with the phase of the moon. Perhaps we just notice the cold more on a clear, moonlit night.

average first frost is on the 4th of September, while in Augusta it's on the 22nd and in Bar Harbor it's in early October. Other towns and cities in the state list additional days when their first freeze is likely. If frost was more likely on a full moon it stands to reason that those dates would be grouped more closely together.

We also know that the lay of the land has a great deal to do with how cold it gets. Just as the heat from the earth is rising on clear nights, the cold air sinks. So people who live in a valley are more likely to have a frost on such nights than those who live on the hillside. You might have even seen that low gardens in your yard will be frosted while other beds are not.

Moon myth-busters are fond of saying that it's likely this belief began because clear, full moon nights make an impression on us. Over the ages, humans have marked the passage of time and the seasons by the phases of the moon and the full moon determines many religious calendars and celebrations. Perhaps as the seasons change, the full moon just seems more *important*.

Did You Know...

Many cultures and traditions give a special name to the full moon of each month. Here are some of them:

January: "Wolf Moon"
February: "Snow Moon"
March: "Sap Moon"
April: "Seed Moon"
May: "Flower Moon"
June: "Rose Moon"
July: "Hay Moon"
August: "Sturgeon Moon"
September: "Harvest Moon"
October: "Hunter's Moon"
November: "Frosty Moon"
December: "Long Nights Moon"

If gardeners named the full moon, I think they would be something like this:

January: "Seed Catalog Moon"
February: "Internet Plant Shopping Moon"
March: "First Trips to Garden Center Moon"
April: "Plant Lust Moon"
May: "Dirty Fingernails Moon"
June: "Still Have Plants Waiting to go in Garden Moon"
July: "Crabgrass Explosion Moon"
August: "Ripe Homegrown Tomatoes! Moon"
September: "Houseplants Back Indoors Moon"
October: "Frost Kill Sadness/Relief Moon"
November: "Pleased Not to be Weeding Moon"
December: "Long Nights Moon"

65. Trees and shrubs grow roots from their trunks and stems.

People who have grown tomato plants know that when you place the plant in the garden you can bury the stem in order to quickly create a deeper root system. Tomatoes will develop roots from their stems and don't suffer when planted several inches deeper than they were grown as seedlings.

Perhaps you've also seen roots grow from forsythia or pussy willow branches that you've put indoors in a vase of water. Sometimes all that's needed to grow new willow or forsythia bushes is to stab a branch into damp soil. Gardeners frequently root slips of plants by placing pieces in water, and amateurs or professionals alike propagate plants from cuttings.

Most plants have the ability to form what are called adventitious roots from other shoot tissues. Some plants will form roots from their trunks or stems, others can form roots from leaves. You may have stuck a leaf from an African violet, jade plant, or begonia into soil and raised an entirely new houseplant from that foliage.

So, if these plants can develop new root systems in such a manner, it seems logical to assume that all plants might benefit from being planted with a portion of their trunk or stems buried. A deeper root system might be good for them all, right? But what is good for some is not good for all plants in all situations.

> There are times when plants actually suffer if their stems are buried too deeply.

There are times when plants actually suffer if their stems are buried too deeply. This is most notable with trees and shrubs. Instead of developing a deeper root system when their trunks are covered with soil, these plants often sulk or die.

How do you know if the plant you're placing in the ground will respond poorly to being planted too deeply? In general, trees and shrubs don't want their stems to be covered because their roots naturally want to be near the top of the soil. When in doubt, look for what's called the root flare and make sure that this is seen above the surface of the ground. The root flare is the area of the trunk that spreads outward into the roots. If a tree's trunk goes straight into the soil and doesn't curve out at the soil line that's an indication that the root flare has been covered and the tree is planted too deeply.

Shrubs that grow with a single trunk, such as rhododendrons, are also sensitive about being too deep. Rhododendrons are single-stemmed plants, and the root flare should be visible above the soil surface. Shrubs that grow from several canes out of the ground, such as forsythia and the big leaf hydrangea, aren't as touchy about planting depth.

When planting a new shrub or tree, move the soil away from the trunk or main stem until you see the root flare, then plant at that depth. Be aware that balled and burlaped plants might have had soil pushed up over the root flare in the process of digging and bagging, so push the soil away from the trunk until you see that outward curve.

Don't worry when the top of roots on older trees are exposed above the soil. Trees' roots want to be in the top few inches of the soil and it's natural as the roots get larger for some of them to appear on the surface.

Plant most perennials at the same depth that they're growing in the container or in their previous location. If an annual or perennial is sturdy in its pot it is likely to be strong once established in the ground as well, so a deeper planting isn't usually necessary.

Many plants can grow roots from branches or stems, but that doesn't mean that it's better to sink them deeper into the soil.

This lovely Stewartia tree clearly shows the flare where the trunk transitions into the roots at soil level. It's not always this pronounced, and on younger trees it may not be prominent, but with close evaluation it's usually noticeable.

66. Put mothballs around the garden to repel pests.

I'm going to call this the reverse-Nike myth. I have always thought that the Nike slogan, *"Just do it"* was advertising brilliance. The motto for mothballs in the garden, however, should be the opposite of the shoe company's catchphrase. Don't do it. Please, please don't do it.

Years ago, when lots of winter clothing was made of wool people would pack those woolens away once spring returned. Sweaters, wool slacks or skirts, scarves and hats would go into

> Do not repeat this myth without adding these three words: don't do it.

storage boxes or bags. Before they were put away, mothballs would be added so that the clothing wouldn't get eaten over the summer. The worst part of this process was when the winter clothes were taken out of storage the following fall. The smell of mothballs would cling to the woolens for days, and the odor wasn't pleasant.

Not only do mothballs stink, they actually smell toxic. It's no wonder people have decided that this readily available, noxious little marble would be perfect for repelling just about anything with a sense of smell.

In the past most mothballs were made of naphthalene. Because this is very flammable, it is banned in some parts of the world and most modern mothballs are now made of other slightly less flammable substances. The new mothballs are equally toxic, however, and there is some concern that both formulations may be a carcinogenic.

Mothballs are designed to be used in enclosed places that will contain the fumes. The packages caution against placing them in open areas where people might inhale the vapors. They are

Sometimes critters make themselves at home where they're not wanted. Mothballs aren't the answer, however, and can actually be more problematic than the wildlife.

a neurotoxin, and although both the odor and this knowledge repels us, there's no evidence that squirrels, skunks, groundhogs, or other critters care one way or the other or are repulsed by the smell.

In addition to being ineffective as an animal repellant, it's irresponsible to throw mothballs out into the environment because they're so poisonous. Animals, especially crows, have been known to pick mothballs up and carry them to other locations. We can't know where they are dropped and who might pick them up.

Do not repeat this myth without adding these three words: *don't do it*.

Did You Know...

There are less toxic means of repelling animal pests. Here are some options:

- Squirrels don't like cayenne pepper. Buy a big jar and sprinkle it on plants or buildings that squirrels are going after. There are squirrel deterrent sprays that are made of cayenne, and birdseed is available that is coated with enough hot pepper that squirrels leave it alone.

- Woodchucks are fairly fastidious animals and don't like it if their tunnels are contaminated with another animal's poop. Who can blame them? It doesn't kill them, but you can get a woodchuck to move elsewhere by dumping cat or dog excrement down their holes.

- Skunks are repelled by ammonia. If a skunk is living under your shed or porch, try soaking some cotton rags or paper towels in ammonia and using a stick to poke them under the structure. Be forewarned: if you do this at night while the skunk is out foraging you're less likely to be sprayed.

- There are motion-activated sprinklers available that repel all sorts of critters, from crows to deer. Attach one of these onto a garden hose and adjust the motion sensor to the size of the animal you're interested in deterring. When the critter in question comes near, the sprinkler lets loose with a sudden burst of water.

- Shiny things that move in a light breeze are often effective at repelling animals. Aluminum pie tins on strings, old silver compact discs, metallic helium balloons and silver streamers have been used to keep birds and problem animals away from the garden.

- Although you'll read that scented soap and human hair will repel deer, these aren't effective for very long. Spray repellants, sprinklers, Wireless Deer Fence, or other common deer fencing are all more successful for controlling Bambi.

67. Fall is the best time to plant and transplant.

The truth will out, all that glitters is not gold, parting is such sweet sorrow – and fall is for planting. Although most people are familiar with the first three phrases, many don't realize that they either originate with or were popularized by William Shakespeare. The last cliché wasn't coined by the Bard of Avon, however. It was part of a fall planting campaign created by the nursery industry.

Not that this slogan is any less true than the others. Fall can be for planting. Since I'm an out-of-control plant person, I will admit that I've put plants in the ground in just about every month of the year and frequently urge others to do the same. Plants bring us so much joy; why should we limit the pleasure we receive from them to only a few months of the year?

The problem is that the fall planting campaign was so successful that many now think fall is the best time to plant or transplant, no matter where you are or what you're growing. Unfortunately, it's not so simple.

On the one hand, early fall can be a great time to move plants and install new ones. The ground is usually still warm and this stimulates roots to grow. The plants aren't pushing as much stem and leaf growth at this time of year so they don't need the same amount of water or other resources as would be required in the summer. And it is usually more pleasant for the gardener to work outdoors in the cooler fall temperatures.

> Fall can be for planting, but it's not that simple.

But there may also be good reasons to wait for spring. Here are a few things to consider about fall transplanting and planting.

Are you going to continue watering these plants for at least two or three months? Although people often think of the fall as a time when rain returns, precipitation isn't necessarily reliable in autumn. Many people turn off their hoses in the fall and forget about irrigation once it gets cooler, but recently installed or transplanted plants will need watering. It's especially important to water newly planted evergreens, as their leaves will be losing moisture all winter long.

When adding to the landscape we should always look for the best plant for the job. In the rush to "get something in the ground" some people buy whatever is left in the nursery in autumn, even if it will soon grow too large or isn't especially hardy. Most nurseries have their best selection of plants in the spring, so sometimes we're well served to wait and choose the most appropriate plantings then.

You'll most likely be successful moving deciduous plants in the fall, but it's preferable to wait and move evergreen plants in the spring.

In general, transplanting earlier in the fall is better than later. This is especially true in areas where cold weather and frozen ground arrive early.

Fall plantings benefit from an application of dark mulch or compost spread around the base of the plant. Cover the root system and at least a foot beyond with an inch or two of mulch; the dark color will absorb some heat from the sun, keeping the ground warmer longer.

Sometimes the truth stays buried: that which glitters might be gold, parting can mean good riddance to bad rubbish, and depending on several factors, fall could be for planting.

Sure, fall is for planting...as is spring, summer, and even winter, depending on the circumstances. Let the plants, weather, and your ability to water be your guide.

68

Beat a non-blooming plant with a rolled-up newspaper.

Artist and gardener Gordon Gaskill swore that threatening his wisteria finally brought it into bloom. He'd been told to hit the plant with a rolled newspaper, but that didn't work. After several years of rampant growth with no flowers, he went out under the arbor and gave the vine an ultimatum. "Bloom next spring or you're out of here." The plant bloomed the following season.

Those with non-blooming wisteria or fruit trees are likely to be told to hit the trunk with a rolled up newspaper or even a board. "*Bad* plant! *Bad* plant!" The theory is that a good beating will shock the plant into blooming. In most cases, this thrashing might release a gardener's frustration, but it's usually a waste of time when it comes to flowering.

It's true that environmental stresses can sometimes bring a plant into bloom. Professional growers have experimented with saline watering, altering hours of daylight and simulating drought as a way to prompt a different flowering pattern. Homeowners might observe a tree that normally blooms in the spring burst into autumnal flowers after the salt and wind from a fall hurricane.

> Delayed blooming might be a result of age, not recalcitrance.

But before adding a rolled-up newspaper to your arsenal of gardening tools, consider that there might be other factors at work. With flowering trees such as crabapples and wisteria vines, delayed blooming is likely to be a result of age, not recalcitrance.

Plants, like people, have a juvenile period during which time they can't reproduce. For some plants this is a matter of weeks and for others it's years. In general, larger plants have longer juvenile stages.

For years, people have been selecting varieties with shorter juvenile periods and finding ways to bring plants into flower and fruit earlier, but there are some that just can't be rushed. If the wisteria or fruit tree is too young, hitting it won't stimulate bloom.

Like Gordon, you can try threats, but it's likely that his wisteria had just grown old enough to flower.

Should a rolled up newspaper be in your store of gardening equipment? Some say a non-flowering plant should be beaten to "shock it into blooming." Instead of a sound thrashing, perhaps it's better to try and figure out why the plant isn't flowering as it should.

69.

Propagate moss by mixing it in a blender with buttermilk, yogurt or beer, and pour it where you want moss to grow.

When you think about growing most plants, a kitchen blender isn't exactly the first gardening tool that comes to mind. So it's no wonder that this method of propagating moss is memorable. But does it work?

I've made an assortment of blended moss cocktails, with and without buttermilk, beer and yogurt. Although some have looked good enough to drink, none have produced a stand of the living plant. Was my technique wrong, or are mosses plants that prefer not to be blended, shaken or stirred?

Who better to comment on this myth than someone who grows mosses professionally. Suzanne Campeau is a biologist and owner of Bryophyta Technologies Inc. (www.bryophyta.ca), a company in Québec that cultivates and sells carpets of moss. The name of her business, Bryophyta, comes from the word bryophytes, which is the division of plants that includes mosses.

The emerald mats that Suzanne grows are sold for landscapes, sculptures or other creative

> Mother Nature doesn't rush to the dairy case when she wants to grow mosses.

projects. And no, Bryophyta does not mix their moss in blenders, nor are there truckloads of yogurt and beer delivered for production.

"As a biologist with a research background," Suzanne says, "I find it very difficult to give an opinion on a method I have not tried thoroughly myself…especially for a book! I tried once to mix mosses and yogurt in a blender and pasted the resulting mixture on a rock, only to find a few days later that some critters had licked my rock clean."

"Over the years I've met a few people who claimed they had success with this method, but a larger number who said they did not. Mosses can regenerate new individuals from pieces of stems or branches, so there is some potential for success. In my opinion this success would highly depend on what species of mosses are used, where they are placed, and how they are pampered in order to grow."

Perhaps that was where I went wrong…I didn't pamper my moss sufficiently after it was poured from the blender. In any case, the addition of buttermilk, beer and yogurt remains suspicious. After all, Mother Nature doesn't rush to the dairy case when she wants to grow mosses, and I'm pretty sure she doesn't pour perfectly good beer onto the ground.

Keep the buttermilk, beer and yogurt in the refrigerator, and follow nature's lead. We know that mosses love moisture, so part of the pampering that Suzanne mentioned is frequent watering. If you've broken off small pieces of mosses (no need for a blender) and placed them where you want moss to grow, misting the area daily will help nurture this plant along.

Once you've watered your bryophytes daily and the tiny plants begin to flourish, expect them

In truth, a blender is apt to puree moss into pieces so small that they're likely to dry out before growing. Transplanting larger pieces of moss, and then keeping them moist with daily watering, is more likely to be successful.

to grow slowly. After you have patiently culti-vated a lovely moss garden, by all means break out the blender. Better to use it for blending celebratory cocktails – without the moss. Cheers!

Did You Know...

- There are more than 12,000 recognized spe-cies of mosses in 700 genera. They are found from the tropics to the poles in all sorts of con-ditions including deserts and along running water.

- In Japanese gardens mosses are cultivated by eliminating their competition. Because mosses are small they can be overrun easily. Daily removal of the smallest of weeds and all debris that falls on top of the mosses is the traditional way to encourage moss growth.

- There are two main types of mosses that peo-ple cultivate, acrocarpous and pleurocarpous. Acrocarpous plants grow upright in cushions or clumps. Pleurocarpous mosses are creepers that tend to spread as carpets instead of tufts.

- Mosses are survivors! A team of scientists from the University of Alberta recently brought some 400-year-old frozen mosses back to life. The team, led by Dr. Catherine La Farge, selected mosses that had been frozen during the last Ice Age and successfully regenerated four species that had spent nearly 400 years beneath a glacier.

70. Put a poinsettia in a dark closet for several weeks in order to get it to bloom again.

One Saturday in August, I was behind the microphone, hosting GardenLine. "Let's talk to Jane," I said, punching the button to put her on the air.

"Oh hi, C.L.," the caller answered, "I'm wondering if you think that it's time for my poinsettia to come out of the closet."

I looked though the studio glass at my board operator, and I could tell by his grin that we were thinking the same thing. *How do you know that poinsettia is gay?*

I didn't say it. "How long has the plant been in the closet," I countered.

"Oh, about six months," Jane replied. "I put it there last March when it started to lose its color. I've heard that they need to spend their off-season in darkness."

We joked about half a year in solitary confinement being harsh punishment for the plant's natural fading. Then I explained that although a dark period was important for the plant's coloration, she was just a *wee bit* off on the timing.

What appear to be flowers on a poinsettia are the bracts that surround the actual bloom. These bracts color-up to form an eye-catching landing pad that lures in pollinators. The real flowers are fairly insignificant in appearance. Yes, the coloration of these bracts depends on a longer period of darkness – but it's hours, not months.

> A dark period is important for the plant's coloration, but it's hours, not months that are required.

In order for the bracts to develop their color the plant needs sunny days alternated with fourteen hours of darkness. This schedule of light and dark must continue for about two months. Even illumination from a lamp or a streetlight outside will delay or prevent coloration.

Some people put their plant in the closet in the early evening, while others cover the plant with an upside down wastebasket, cardboard box or other light-blocking object. If you have a southern or west-facing room with absolutely no lights inside or outside, the poinsettia can be kept in the window there. It will color in this location but it might not be beautiful for the holidays.

When saving this holiday plant from year to year, be sure to repot and fertilize it regularly. Homegrown poinsettias tend to be a bit "leaner and meaner" than greenhouse grown plants. But if you want big, lush and gorgeous there is nothing like one that's been commercially grown.

Because this poinsettia is variegated you can see how the leaves just below the red bracts also begin to color at this time of year. Even without the red tops, this variety would be lovely outdoors, planted for foliage interest in the summer. Although I'll put this outside in a garden or container, I won't be likely to provide the hours of darkness needed to turn the bracts red before the holidays.

Did You Know...

The Long Lasting Poinsettia

Once a flower is pollinated, its job of attracting pollinators is done, so it usually wilts. The colorful Poinsettia stays bright for months because it's the bracts that are eye catching, not the blossoms. Bracts are specialized leaves right underneath the actual flowers and they keep their color even after the flowers are pollinated and gone.

The Point of its Name

Although many people commonly say "point-setta" or shorten the name to "points," there is no "point" in poinsettia. This is a plant that is so associated with its common name that few use the botanical label *Euphorbia pulcherrima*.

Historian and writer William Prescott proposed poinsettia as the plant's popular name. Joel Roberts Poinsett was the first United States Ambassador to Mexico in the 1820s. He was an amateur botanist and took cuttings from a shrub he came across while in Mexico, bringing them back to his greenhouse in South Carolina.

Cut Flowers

In the early 1900s, the Ecke family raised poinsettias for use as cut flowers and landscape plants. These Southern California growers saw the potential of this *Euphorbia* as a holiday plant and are responsible for the development and popularization of the poinsettias we love today. Although we now think of these as indoor plants, not as florist flowers, if a branch or two breaks off of your plant don't throw it away! Place them in a vase or use in an arrangement with evergreens and other clippings from the winter garden.

71. I tried it and it worked, so it must be true.

This is the fiction that propagates many garden myths. It's also known as, "Well, it worked for *me*."

> There is a notion that if it's old it must be wise.

This message was hung on the wishing tree at the Berkshire Botanic Garden in Stockbridge, Mass. May we always enter our yards and gardens with such an astute approach.

People will say that they put the plant on its side or turned it upside down. They cut it back or didn't cut it back. They applied this unusual product or used that timing. Lo and behold, the plant did just what they wanted it to do! Their actions clearly worked, right?

That's like saying that we danced naked around the maypole and spring came, so prancing in the nude around a post must bring winter to an end. Or, that she sang the national anthem while planting this group of daffodils and they flowered better than all the others, so the song must stimulate narcissus growth. True, these are silly examples, but that's the kind of thinking that gets applied to garden practices.

Because you did "A" and then saw "B" does not necessarily mean that "A" caused "B."

When we've tried a practice or product and the plant did well this doesn't mean that there was a direct

cause and effect going on. And just because we've seen something work once doesn't mean that the same results will be replicated in the future.

Plants want to live and grow, and often they do so despite our help, not because of it. Conversely, sometimes we do everything right and our plant still dies.

For some reason, people are attracted to novel solutions. I'm reminded of a phrase that's currently seen all over the Internet. Ads talk about "this old weird tip" or "weird old trick." These words are used to sell everything from weight loss products to wrinkle creams. The fact that this phrasing is repeated so frequently tells us that it must be successful in driving traffic to those sites. There is a notion that if it's old it must be wise, and if it's weird it will also be fun!

We humans want to believe that there is some quirky, easy method to getting what we want. Yet time and again we see that some tips and tricks aren't helpful, and weird is usually just strange.

Here's the latest dirt: it may not be unusual or easy, but the best old standbys are hard work, common sense, an open mind and the scientific method.

Make your garden ornaments as eccentric as you wish, but keep your remedies in harmony with the natural world.

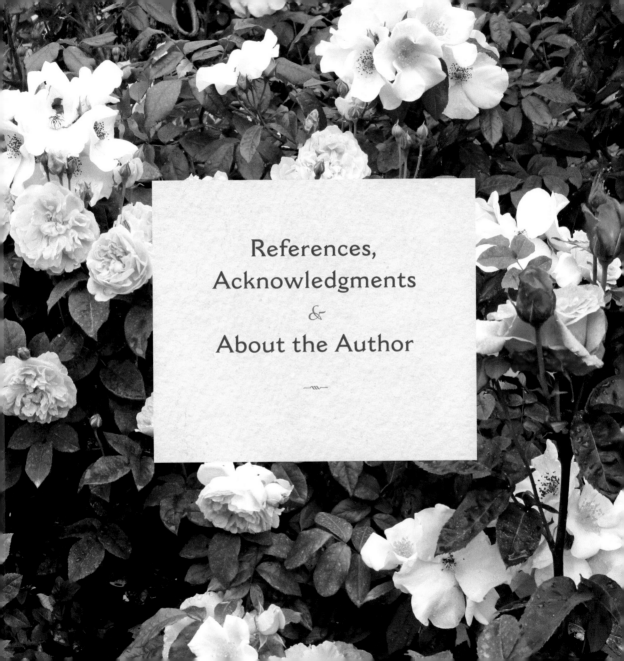

References,
Acknowledgments
&
About the Author

References

My search for the roots of common garden myths was made possible in part by the Library of Congress. Their website Chronicling America allows a computer search of newspapers from all over the U.S. At this writing, papers that were published between 1836 and 1922 are available. http://chroniclingamerica.loc.gov/

I also had the pleasure of referring to the following older books. Some of them have been digitally scanned and are available in print once again.

Bailey, L.H. (1911) *Farm and Garden Rule-Book.* New York: The Macmillan Company

Glenny, George (1880). *A Year's Work in Garden and Greenhouse.* London: Chatto and Windus, Piccadilly

Greiner, T. (1894) *How to Make the Garden Pay.* Philadelphia: W. Henry Maule

Henderson, Peter (1910). *Henderson's Handbook of Plants and General Horticulture.* New York: Peter Henderson & Company

Loudon, J.W. (1853) *The Ladies' Companion to The Flower-Garden.* London: Bradbury & Evans

Parsons, Samuel Jr. (1895) *Landscape Gardening.* New York, London: The Knickerbocker Press

Thomas, H. H. (Editor) (1910). *Gardening Difficulties Solved.* London: Cassell and Company, LTD

Recommended Reading For Those Who Want to Dig Deeper

There are more myths about gardening than just about any other subject except, possibly, weight loss. If you'd like to read more about common garden lore and misinformation you'll enjoy these wonderful books:

The Informed Gardener and *The Informed Gardener Blooms Again,* by Linda Chalker-Schott, published by University of Washington Press.

Decoding Garden Advice, The Truth About Garden Remedies, and *The Truth about Organic Gardening,* by Jeff Gillman, published by Timber Press.

Acknowledgments

*W*hether you're cultivating a career, children or a garden, the more willing helpers you have, the better the results. So it is with a book. Without the following people, *Coffee for Roses* wouldn't have been possible. With great affection and gratitude for all, I thank these individuals.

Dan Fornari, my family and friends. You have all been continually supportive; I never take this for granted and constantly value what a gift you are.

Wallace Exman, a consummate publishing professional, thought I could be an author and asked me to write a book. If I ever need an example of the way that one person can have a transformative and positive effect on the lives of others, I need to look no further than Wally.

Greg and Pat Williams published *HortIdeas* for many years; in that time I relied on their careful reading and reporting of plant science journals to help keep me informed. The research behind several of the myths in this book was brought to my attention in their monthly publications.

Many fellow writers, garden communicators and horticultural professionals have been generous beyond measure; I am continually edified by your knowledge and assistance. Particular thanks go to those who provided information, feedback and quotes for this book.

I'm also grateful to the kind plant lovers who have allowed me to photograph their plants and gardens. The Garden Writers Association also deserves a shout-out for facilitating visits to superb public and private gardens in conjunction with their meetings.

My heartfelt appreciation goes to Paul Kelly, Cathy Dees, Holly Rosborough, and the rest of the staff at St Lynn's Press. I am only one of many who value their support, professional guidance and hard work, and applaud their continued focus on plants and gardening.

The proverb says that many hands make light work, but it's also true that many hands grow beautiful gardens.

About the Author

C.L. Fornari is a plant geek who fell into garden communications because of her desire to introduce others to the joys of plants and gardening. She is the author six books, including *Your Garden Shouldn't Make You Crazy*, *A Garden Wedding* and *A Garden Lover's Martha's Vineyard*. She's been a monthly columnist for *Angie's List Magazine* and *Prime Time Magazine* and contributed numerous articles to other publications, including *American Nurseryman*.

For the past thirteen years C.L. has hosted GardenLine, a live two-hour call-in radio show on WXTK that is streamed online on www.95WXTK.com . Before that, she was a weekly contributor to The Cultivated Gardener, heard on NPR stations nationwide. In 2012, C.L. was awarded the Garden Communicator prize from the Perennial Plant Association, and in 2013, her work online and on the radio won three awards of excellence from the Garden Writers Association.

C.L. speaks to a variety of audiences ranging from green industry trade shows to garden clubs and alumni associations. She is dedicated to giving garden center employees and landscapers information they can use to better promote and expand their businesses, and to providing home landscapers with the information they need to be successful in their yards and gardens.

In addition to speaking, radio and her own writing, she blogs and runs a consultation service for Hyannis Country Garden, an independent garden center on Cape Cod. C.L. has gardened in Southern California, Wisconsin, and Upstate New York; and now she grows all manner of plants at Poison Ivy Acres, her home on Cape Cod.

Look for her online at www.GardenLady.com and www.CoffeeForRoses.com.